Shark Savvy: The Tank-Tested Playbook for Entrepreneurial Domination Book Series

https://www.amazon.com/gp/product/B0DCH21VC9

by Shark Savvy (Author) , Jimmy Slagle (Author)

Welcome to the Shark Savvy series, where we turn Shark Tank episodes into your personal MBA program—minus the soul-crushing debt and questionable cafeteria food.

Picture this: You're lounging on your couch, binge-watching Shark Tank, when suddenly you realize you've learned more about business in one hour than you did in four years of college. That's the Shark Savvy experience, but on steroids (the legal kind, we promise).

Each book in this groundbreaking series takes a deep dive into a single Shark Tank episode, extracting the juiciest, most mind-blowing business lessons that most entrepreneurs miss while they're distracted by Mr. Wonderful's dazzling bald head. We're talking real, actionable insights that you can apply to your business faster than Mark Cuban can say, "I'm out."

But wait, there's more! (Yes, we went there.) These books aren't just educational—they're more entertaining than watching Kevin O'Leary try to dance. We've infused each page with wit sharper than Lori Greiner's negotiation skills and wisdom more profound than Daymond John's fashion sense.

Here's what you're in for with each Shark Savvy book:

1. A blow-by-blow analysis of a Shark Tank pitch that'll make you feel like you're right there in the Tank (minus the intimidating cameras and Barbara Corcoran's penetrating stare).
2. Mind-bending business lessons that'll have you slapping your forehead and saying, "Why didn't I think of that?" (Don't slap too hard; we need your brain cells intact.)
3. Practical exercises that'll whip your entrepreneurial muscles into shape faster than you can say "royalty deal."
4. Real-world applications that'll help you swim with the sharks instead of becoming chum.
5. A healthy dose of Stoic philosophy, because nothing says "I'm a serious entrepreneur" like quoting Marcus Aurelius while pitching your avocado toast food truck.

The content presented on sharksavvy.com and its affiliates, including our social media channels, references the television show "Shark Tank." "Shark Tank" is a registered trademark of ABC and Sony Pictures Television. The material provided here is for educational and informational purposes only. It aims to offer commentary, analysis, and insights based on personal observations and experiences. In accordance with the principles of fair use, brief excerpts from "Shark Tank" are used to illustrate specific points and provide context for the discussion. These references are employed in a transformative manner, adding new meaning, understanding, and educational value beyond the original content. This work is not affiliated with, endorsed by, or sponsored by "Shark Tank," ABC, Sony Pictures Television, or any of their associated entities. All rights to the original material are owned by their respective copyright holders. For more information on fair use, please consult legal resources or seek professional legal advice.

Disclaimer: This book is based on real Shark Tank pitches, but let's be real—we're not fortune tellers or miracle workers. The advice in this book is for entertainment and educational purposes only. We've done our best to provide solid, actionable insights, but we can't guarantee you'll become the next Mark Cuban just by reading it (though we'd love to take credit if you do).

The stories and examples in this book are based on actual Shark Tank episodes, but we've taken some creative liberties to make them more entertaining and educational. Any resemblance to actual persons, living or dead, or actual events is purely coincidental—except when it isn't.

Remember, swimming with sharks can be dangerous. Always consult with qualified professionals before making important business decisions. We're not responsible for any financial losses, bruised egos, or sudden urges to pitch your ideas to strangers on the street.

Now, let's dive in and start making some waves in the business world!

Are You Ready To Become Shark Savvy?

We invite you to subscribe to our Free Newsletter - The Shark Savvy Stoic. 3 times a week (Monday, Wednesday, and Friday) we send you some savvy wisdom that we have uncovered during our Shark Tank Pitch evaluations. And if you join us today we will include a digital copy of The Entrepreneur's Eureka: A 5-Question Interactive Workbook. Dive into the minds of Shark Tank's most successful investors with this powerful, interactive workbook. Uncover the five critical questions that can turn any business scenario into a goldmine of insights. Inside, you'll find:

- A step-by-step framework to analyze business situations like a pro
- Real-world examples from Shark Tank's biggest success stories
- Practical exercises to immediately apply to your own ventures
- A self-assessment tool to measure your "Shark Savvy" quotient
- An action plan template to turn insights into tangible results turn insights into tangible results

Join Us Here: https://sharksavvy.com/s15e1

But here's the kicker: Each book stands alone as a complete guide to entrepreneurial badassery. However, collect them all, and you'll have a library of business wisdom more valuable than a 20% stake in Amazon circa 1997.

So, why should you buy every book in the Shark Savvy series? Because in the cutthroat world of business, you need every advantage you can get. It's like Pokemon for entrepreneurs—gotta catch 'em all if you want to be the very best (like no one ever was).

Whether you're a seasoned business owner looking to up your game or a wide-eyed newbie who thinks a "liquidation event" involves spring break in Cancun, the Shark Savvy series has something for you. Each book is a treasure trove of lessons, laughs, and "let's do this" motivation that'll have you revamping your business plan before you've even finished the epilogue.

Don't let your entrepreneurial dreams become the one that got away. Dive into the Shark Savvy series and start your journey from guppy to great white today. Remember, in the vast ocean of business, it's eat or be eaten—and we're serving up a feast of knowledge that's sure to satisfy even the hungriest of entrepreneurs.

So what are you waiting for? Grab your scuba gear (or just your reading glasses) and plunge into the Shark Savvy series. Your future self—you know, the one sipping margaritas on your private island—will thank you.

Shark Savvy: Because why learn from your own mistakes when you can learn from someone else's on national television?
Want to go even Deeper? Check out SharkSavvy.com and Dive Into The Depths of Success!

Lesson 3. The Timing Tightrope: Navigating the Gap Between Concept and Proof

Introduction: When Pizza Met Its Match

The Unexpected Pairing: Pizza and Wine Reimagined

Setting the Stage: Kevin and Joshua's Journey to the Tank

Three Game-Changing Lessons for Niche Product Entrepreneurs

Lesson 1: The Hyper-Niche Gambit: Slicing the Market Pie

Defining the Pizza-Wine Connection

The Power and Pitfalls of Hyper-Niche Marketing

"Expanding Your Slice"

Strategies for Broadening Appeal Without Losing Core Identity

Action Plan: Crafting a Scalable Niche Product Narrative

Lesson 2: The All-In Entrepreneur: Betting the House (Literally)

Skin in the Game: When Founders Go All-In

The Double-Edged Sword of Personal Investment

"Balancing Passion and Pragmatism"

Tactics for Demonstrating Commitment Without Raising Red Flags

Checklist: Smart Personal Investment Strategies for Startups

Lesson 3: The Timing Tango: Dancing Between Concept and Proof

The Critical Window of Investment Opportunity

Navigating the No-Man's Land Between Idea and Market Validation

"Bridging the Proof Gap"

Techniques for Building Credibility in Early-Stage Ventures

personal struggle into a business idea

4. "Multi-Sensory Pitch Deck": Create a pitch that engages all five senses

Are You Ready To Become Shark Savvy?

Shark Savvy: The Tank-Tested Playbook for Entrepreneurial Domination Book Series

Pitch 1: Gatsby Chocolate

Gatsby Chocolate: The Sweet Revolution

In a thrilling Shark Tank episode, brothers Ryan and Doug, known as Raj and Dodge, stepped into the tank with a revolutionary product that promised to transform the chocolate industry. Their pitch for Gatsby Chocolate was not just about a new candy bar; it was about reinventing indulgence.

- **Product Name:** Gatsby Chocolate
- **Pitch Summary:** A healthier chocolate alternative with significantly reduced calories and sugar, without compromising on taste.
- **Founders:** Ryan (Raj) and Doug (Dodge)
- **Product Summary:** Gatsby Chocolate offers a range of chocolate products with up to 75% less sugar and about half the calories of traditional chocolates, maintaining a rich, satisfying taste.
- **Category:** Food & Beverage / Health Conscious Snacks
- **Deal Requested:** $500,000 for 5% equity
- **Offer Made:** Yes
- **Offer Terms:** Multiple offers were made, with negotiations leading to a final offer.
- **Deal Accepted:** Yes
- **Deal Terms:** $500,000 (half as equity, half as a loan) for 20% equity, with additional equity triggers at sales milestones.

- **Deal Sharks:** Lori Greiner and Mark Cuban

The brothers, leveraging their success from founding Halo Top ice cream, presented Gatsby Chocolate as the "Halo Top of Chocolate." With national distribution in major retailers like Walmart and Safeway, and over 6,000 points of distribution, Gatsby Chocolate had already made significant inroads into the market.

The pitch took an unexpected turn when the Sharks tasted the product, unanimously praising its flavor despite the reduced calorie and sugar content. However, concerns were raised about the branding and packaging, which sparked a heated discussion about the product's market positioning.

As negotiations unfolded, the brothers demonstrated their entrepreneurial acumen, openly discussing their challenges and their need for strategic partnerships to achieve national awareness. This transparency, combined with their track record and the product's potential, ultimately led to a deal with Lori Greiner and Mark Cuban.

The final agreement not only provided the requested capital but also secured valuable partnerships that could potentially transform Gatsby Chocolate from a promising startup into a household name. As the brothers left the Tank, it was clear that this sweet deal could be the beginning of a new revolution in the chocolate industry.

The Art of the Sweet Deal: Why Gatsby Chocolate Scored Big

The Gatsby Chocolate pitch resulted in a successful deal, showcasing several key factors that appealed to the Sharks. Let's break down the elements that led to this sweet success:

1. **Proven Track Record**: The founders' history with Halo Top, a wildly successful brand in the better-for-you ice cream category, lent significant credibility to their new venture. This past success demonstrated their ability to disrupt and innovate in the food industry.
2. **Product Quality**: All Sharks were impressed by the taste of Gatsby Chocolate, despite its reduced calorie and sugar content. This validation of the product's quality was crucial in generating interest and confidence in its market potential.
3. **Market Traction**: With over 6,000 points of distribution in major national retailers like Walmart and Safeway, Gatsby Chocolate had already proven its ability to secure shelf space and generate sales.
4. **Innovative Product**: The chocolate bars filled a gap in the market for healthier indulgence options, aligning with current consumer trends towards healthier eating without sacrificing taste.

5. **Intellectual Property**: The mention of a patent-pending formula added value to the company's long-term potential and defensibility in the market.
6. **Transparency and Humility**: The founders were open about their challenges, particularly in achieving national awareness. This honesty and recognition of their limitations appealed to the Sharks, who saw an opportunity to add value.
7. **Flexibility in Negotiations**: The founders demonstrated willingness to adjust their equity offer and consider creative deal structures, showing their commitment to securing a strategic partnership.
8. **Growth Potential**: Despite current losses, the Sharks saw potential for significant growth and profitability improvement, especially with their guidance and resources.
9. **Brand Potential**: While the current branding was criticized, the Sharks recognized the opportunity to reshape and elevate the brand, particularly with Lori's expertise in this area.
10. **Strategic Fit**: The deal aligned with the Sharks' interests and expertise, particularly Lori's experience in retail products and branding, and Mark's broad business acumen.

Entrepreneurs can learn several valuable lessons from this pitch:

- Leverage past successes to build credibility for new ventures.
- Ensure product quality is undeniable, especially in competitive markets.

- Secure significant market traction before seeking investment.
- Be transparent about challenges and open to guidance.
- Remain flexible in negotiations to secure strategic partnerships.
- Consider the value of branding and be open to expert input for improvement.
- Demonstrate a clear understanding of your market position and growth potential.

By embodying these principles, Gatsby Chocolate not only secured a deal but also positioned itself for potential market leadership in the healthier indulgence category.

Sweet Revelations: Unconventional Wisdom from Gatsby Chocolate

Lesson 1: The Paradox of Past Success: Embracing Beginner's Mind

Business Lesson: Past success can be both a powerful asset and a dangerous liability. True innovation often requires returning to a beginner's mindset, even after achieving significant success.

Scenario: Ryan and Doug, despite their success with Halo Top, admitted to "romanticizing the early days" and acknowledged the challenges they faced with Gatsby Chocolate. This humility and willingness to start fresh led to their openness to partnerships and guidance from the Sharks.

Entrepreneurial Application: Successful entrepreneurs should cultivate a "beginner's mind" when starting new ventures. This involves:

- Questioning assumptions based on past successes
- Seeking mentorship and partnerships, even if you've "been there before"
- Embracing the learning curve of a new market or product category
- Using past success as a foundation for credibility, not as a blueprint for the new

Lesson 2: The Awareness Arbitrage: Bridging the Gap Between Distribution and Recognition

Business Lesson: In the modern market, securing wide distribution doesn't guarantee success. The real challenge lies in bridging the gap between physical presence and consumer awareness.

Scenario: Gatsby Chocolate had achieved impressive distribution in major retailers, yet lacked national awareness. This disparity highlighted a critical challenge in today's saturated market: the need for strategic marketing and branding to complement physical availability.

Entrepreneurial Application: Entrepreneurs should focus on:

- Developing a two-pronged strategy that balances distribution and brand awareness
- Leveraging strategic partnerships (like with the Sharks) to boost brand recognition
- Creating a strong, cohesive brand identity that stands out on shelves and in consumers' minds
- Utilizing innovative marketing techniques to create buzz around widely distributed products
- Measuring and analyzing the correlation between distribution points and actual sales to identify awareness gaps

Lesson 3: The Ethical Evolution: Navigating Changing Consumer Values in Product Design

Business Lesson: Product design and marketing must evolve with shifting societal values and generational perspectives, particularly around sensitive topics like health and body image.

Scenario: The critique of Gatsby Chocolate's calorie-focused packaging raised important questions about changing attitudes towards diet culture, especially among younger demographics. This insight highlighted the need for brands to stay attuned to evolving societal norms and values.

Entrepreneurial Application: Forward-thinking entrepreneurs should:

- Conduct regular research on changing societal values, particularly among target demographics
- Design products and packaging that align with current ethical and social standards
- Be prepared to pivot branding strategies to resonate with evolving consumer values
- Create marketing messages that focus on positive attributes (e.g., taste, quality ingredients) rather than potentially sensitive metrics (e.g., calorie counts)
- Engage in ongoing dialogue with consumers to understand their changing perspectives and adapt accordingly

- Consider forming ethics advisory boards to guide product development and marketing strategies

These lessons underscore the importance of maintaining humility, bridging the gap between distribution and awareness, and staying attuned to evolving societal values in product design and marketing. By applying these insights, entrepreneurs can navigate the complex landscape of modern business more effectively, creating products that not only reach shelves but also resonate deeply with consumers.

The Chocolate Revolution: Gatsby's Sweet Disruption

Picture this: You're lounging on your couch, craving something sweet. You reach for a chocolate bar, but that nagging voice in your head reminds you of all the sugar and calories. Now, imagine if that voice suddenly fell silent, replaced by a chorus of "go ahead, indulge!" That's the world Gatsby Chocolate is trying to create, and let me tell you, it's a world I want to live in.

When Ryan and Doug (or should I say, Raj and Dodge) strutted into the Shark Tank, they weren't just peddling another candy bar. No, these brothers were selling a revolution wrapped in chocolate. As I watched them pitch Gatsby Chocolate, I couldn't help but feel a sense of déjà vu. Here were two guys who had already turned the ice cream world upside down with Halo Top, now back for round two in the arena of guilty pleasures.

But hold on to your taste buds, because this isn't just another tale of entrepreneurial success. It's a story of redemption, innovation, and the sweet, sweet irony of needing help after you've already made it big.

Gatsby Chocolate isn't just a product; it's a philosophy. It's the crazy idea that you can have your chocolate and eat it too, without sacrificing taste or your waistline. With up to 75% less sugar and about half the calories of traditional chocolates, these bars are like the Navy SEALs of the candy aisle - elite, effective, and defying all odds.

Now, you might be thinking, "Great, another 'healthy' chocolate that probably tastes like cardboard dipped in sadness." But here's where it gets interesting. Even the Sharks, those cold-blooded predators of the business world, were caught off guard by how good this stuff actually tastes. It was like watching a group of hardened food critics suddenly turn into kids on Christmas morning.

But don't let the sweet taste fool you. Behind this chocolatey exterior lies a treasure trove of lessons that could make or break your next venture. We're not just talking about obvious stuff like "make a good product" or "know your market." No, we're diving into the deep end of the entrepreneurial pool, exploring paradoxes that would make even the most seasoned business guru's head spin.

In the pages that follow, we'll unravel three mind-bending insights that emerged from this pitch:

1. Why success can be your worst enemy, and how embracing failure might just be your ticket to the big leagues.
2. The bizarre world where having your product everywhere doesn't mean anyone knows about it, and how to bridge that gap.
3. How slapping a few numbers on a wrapper can turn your health-conscious product into a social pariah, and why understanding shifting cultural values is crucial for your brand's survival.

So, grab your favorite snack (might I suggest a Gatsby Chocolate bar?), get comfortable, and prepare to have your entrepreneurial mind blown. We're about to embark on a journey through the world of health-conscious indulgence, marketing paradoxes, and the rollercoaster ride of starting over after you've already won.

Welcome to the sweet revolution. Things are about to get deliciously complicated.

Lesson 1: The Paradox of Past Success: Embracing Beginner's Mind

Picture this: You're standing atop a mountain you've just conquered, basking in the glory of your achievement. The view is breathtaking, the air is crisp, and you feel invincible. Now, imagine someone telling you that to reach even greater heights, you need to climb back down and start over. Sounds crazy, right? Welcome to the paradox of past success.

When Ryan and Doug sauntered into the Shark Tank with Gatsby Chocolate, they weren't just any entrepreneurs. These were the guys who had already planted their flag at the summit of Mount Success with Halo Top. They'd disrupted the ice cream industry, laughed in the face of sugar, and probably bought a few fancy cars along the way. By all accounts, they should've been experts at this whole "revolutionize a junk food" game.

But here's where it gets interesting. Instead of cocky grins and a "we've got this" attitude, our dynamic duo showed up with a surprising dose of humility. Ryan admitted, and I quote, "I romanticized the early days way too much." It was like watching a master chef confess he'd burned toast.

This, my friends, is the sweet spot where true innovation happens. It's the moment when you realize that your previous victories, as glorious as they were, might just be the very thing holding you back from your next big win.

The Double-Edged Sword of Prior Achievements

Success is intoxicating. It's the business world's equivalent of a sugar high – it feels great in the moment, but too much of it can leave you sluggish and unable to adapt. When you've got a big win under your belt, it's tempting to think you've cracked the code. You start to believe your own hype, and before you know it, you're trying to force-fit old solutions into new problems.

Ryan and Doug could've easily fallen into this trap. They could've approached Gatsby Chocolate with a "Halo Top 2.0" mindset, assuming that what worked for ice cream would automatically work for chocolate. But instead, they did something remarkable – they admitted they needed help.

Rediscovering Humility: The Gatsby Chocolate Story

Watching these successful entrepreneurs humble themselves in front of the Sharks was like seeing a plot twist in a blockbuster movie. It was unexpected, refreshing, and totally changed the game.

By acknowledging their need for guidance, particularly in achieving national awareness, Ryan and Doug opened themselves up to new possibilities. They weren't just seeking money; they were looking for partners who could help them navigate uncharted waters.

This willingness to start fresh, to approach Gatsby Chocolate as a new challenge rather than a repeat performance, is what I call embracing the "beginner's mind." It's about looking at your business with fresh eyes, unburdened by the weight of past successes or failures.

The Power of Unlearning: Strategies for a Fresh Start

So, how do you cultivate this beginner's mind, especially when your resume is already impressive? Here are some strategies to help you unlearn success and rediscover your entrepreneurial mojo:

1. **Question Everything**: Treat your assumptions like a detective grills a suspect. Just because something worked before doesn't mean it's the right solution now.
2. **Seek Diverse Perspectives**: Surround yourself with people who think differently. If you're a tech whiz, buddy up with a creative type. If you're a numbers person, find someone who excels at soft skills.
3. **Embrace Discomfort**: If you're feeling too comfortable, you're probably not growing. Seek out situations that challenge your expertise and force you to adapt.
4. **Celebrate Small Failures**: Each mini-flop is a lesson in disguise. Train yourself to see failures as stepping stones rather than stumbling blocks.
5. **Stay Curious**: Cultivate a genuine interest in learning new things, especially in areas outside your expertise. You never know where your next big idea might come from.

Checklist: Cultivating Beginner's Mind in Your Next Venture

- Identify and list your core assumptions about your business or industry

- Find a mentor or advisor from a completely different field
- Take on a small project in an unfamiliar area of your business
- Set aside time each week for learning something new and unrelated to your primary expertise
- Create a "failure resume" highlighting what you've learned from past mistakes
- Organize regular brainstorming sessions with a diverse group of thinkers
- Practice explaining your business to a child or someone completely unfamiliar with your industry

Remember, the goal isn't to discard your hard-earned wisdom. It's about finding the balance between leveraging your experience and remaining open to new ideas and approaches.

As we saw with Gatsby Chocolate, sometimes the most powerful move you can make is admitting you don't have all the answers. It's about having the courage to climb back down the mountain and start a new ascent, armed with the wisdom of your past climbs but unburdened by the weight of your previous summit flags.

In the end, success isn't just about reaching the top. It's about enjoying the climb, learning from each step, and being willing to explore new peaks, even if it means starting from base camp all over again. After all, in the world of entrepreneurship, the journey is just as sweet as the chocolate at the end of it.

Lesson 2: The Awareness Arbitrage: Bridging the Distribution-Recognition Gap

Picture this: You've just created the world's most amazing chocolate bar. It's sitting on shelves in every major retailer across the country. You should be rolling in dough (both the cash and the cookie variety), right? Wrong. Welcome to the bizarre world of modern business, where being everywhere doesn't necessarily mean being known.

This, my friends, is the conundrum that had Ryan and Doug scratching their heads as they stood before the Sharks. Gatsby Chocolate wasn't just in a few boutique shops or health food stores. No, these low-calorie treats had managed to sweet-talk their way onto the shelves of retail giants like Walmart and Safeway. Over 6,000 points of distribution, to be exact. That's more locations than I have excuses for why I need "just one more" piece of chocolate.

But here's the kicker - despite this impressive reach, Gatsby Chocolate was facing a problem that would make any entrepreneur want to drown their sorrows in a vat of cocoa. They had national distribution without national awareness. It's like throwing the party of the century and forgetting to send out invitations.

The Modern Market Paradox: Shelf Space vs. Mind Space

In the good old days (you know, when dinosaurs roamed the earth and people actually watched cable TV), getting your product into stores was half the battle. If you could secure prime shelf space, you were golden. Customers would stroll down the aisle, see your product, and curiosity (or clever packaging) would do the rest.

Fast forward to today, and we're living in a world where attention is the new currency. We're bombarded with more products, ads, and choices than ever before. In this chaos, simply being present isn't enough. You need to be memorable, to cut through the noise and stake a claim in the consumer's mind.

Gatsby Chocolate found itself smack dab in the middle of this paradox. They'd won the distribution game, but were losing the battle for mindshare. It's like having the world's best megaphone but forgetting to turn it on.

Gatsby's Dilemma: National Distribution Without National Awareness

When Ryan admitted to the Sharks, "We have national distribution without national awareness," you could almost hear the collective "aha" moment. It was a stark reminder that in today's market, physical presence and mental presence are two very different beasts.

This gap between distribution and recognition is what I call the "Awareness Arbitrage." It's the space where savvy entrepreneurs can gain a massive advantage by focusing not just on where their product is, but on how it's perceived and remembered.

For Gatsby Chocolate, this meant realizing that getting on shelves was only the first step. The real challenge lay in getting into shopping carts and, more importantly, into the minds and hearts of consumers.

Beyond the Shelf: Crafting a Holistic Market Presence

So, how do you bridge this gap? How do you turn shelf space into mind space? Here are some strategies to help you navigate this tricky terrain:

1. **Tell a Compelling Story**: Your product isn't just a thing; it's a narrative. Craft a story that resonates with your audience. For Gatsby Chocolate, it could be the tale of guilt-free

indulgence or the underdog challenging big candy.

2. **Leverage Social Proof**: In a world drowning in choices, people look to others for guidance. Encourage and showcase customer reviews, testimonials, and user-generated content.
3. **Create Experiences, Not Just Products**: Think beyond the purchase. How can you create memorable experiences around your brand? Could Gatsby Chocolate partner with gyms for post-workout treats or team up with book clubs for guilt-free reading snacks?
4. **Harness the Power of Micro-Influencers**: Sometimes, a chorus of smaller voices can be more powerful than one loud shout. Find influencers who align with your brand values and can authentically share your story.
5. **Master the Art of Retail Theater**: Make your in-store presence impossible to ignore. Creative displays, interactive elements, or even in-store sampling can turn a passive shopper into an engaged customer.
6. **Align with Larger Movements**: Connect your brand with broader societal trends or movements. Gatsby Chocolate could position itself at the intersection of wellness and indulgence, tapping into the growing "health-ish" movement.

Action Plan: Synchronizing Distribution and Brand Recognition

Ready to close the gap between where you are and who knows about you? Here's a step-by-step plan to get you started:

1. **Audit Your Current Presence:**
   - Map out where your product is available
   - Analyze current brand awareness metrics
   - Identify gaps between distribution and recognition
2. **Define Your Brand Story:**
   - Craft a compelling narrative that goes beyond product features
   - Identify key emotional triggers for your target audience
   - Develop a consistent brand voice across all channels
3. **Create a Multi-Channel Awareness Strategy:**
   - Identify key online and offline channels for your audience
   - Develop tailored content for each channel
   - Set measurable goals for brand awareness and engagement
4. **Activate In-Store Experiences:**
   - Design eye-catching displays or packaging
   - Plan and execute in-store events or sampling programs
   - Train retail staff to become brand ambassadors
5. **Leverage Partnerships and Collaborations:**
   - Identify potential partners who share your target audience
   - Develop co-marketing campaigns or limited-edition products
   - Explore unconventional partnerships that can generate buzz
6. **Measure and Iterate:**

- Set up tracking for both distribution metrics and awareness KPIs
- Regularly analyze the correlation between distribution points and brand recognition
- Be prepared to pivot and adjust strategies based on data

Remember, in the game of Awareness Arbitrage, the goal isn't just to be everywhere – it's to be unforgettable. It's about creating a presence that lingers in the mind long after the shopping trip is over.

For Gatsby Chocolate, and for any brand facing this modern dilemma, the key lies in seeing distribution and awareness not as separate challenges, but as two sides of the same deliciously complex coin. By aligning these elements, you create a brand presence that's not just widespread, but deeply impactful.

In the end, it's not just about being on the shelf; it's about being the brand that customers walk into the store specifically to find. Because when you can turn "Oh, what's this?" into "Oh, I've been looking for this!" – that's when you know you've truly arrived.

Lesson 3: The Ethical Evolution: Aligning Product Design with Changing Values

Picture this: You've created a product that's healthier, tastier, and seemingly perfect for the modern consumer. You've plastered the calories front and center on the packaging, proud of your low-calorie achievement. You're feeling pretty good about yourself, right? Well, buckle up, buttercup, because you might have just stepped into an ethical minefield without even realizing it.

This is exactly the situation our intrepid Gatsby Chocolate founders found themselves in when they faced the Sharks. There they were, proudly showcasing their low-calorie chocolate bars, when BAM! – guest Shark Emma Grede dropped a truth bomb that probably left them feeling like they'd been hit by a truck made of kale smoothies and yoga mats.

"Millennial and Gen Z, they consider this toxic diet culture," Emma pointed out, referring to the prominently displayed calorie count. "And I think there's going to be a backlash against that a little bit."

Just like that, what seemed like a selling point suddenly became a potential liability. Welcome to the wild world of ethical product design in the age of rapidly evolving consumer values.

The Calorie Conundrum: When Good Intentions Backfire

For years, calorie counting was the gold standard of health-conscious eating. Slap a low number on the package, and health-minded consumers would flock to your product like seagulls to a dropped ice cream cone. It was simple, straightforward, and seemed like a no-brainer for a brand positioning itself as a healthier alternative.

But here's the thing about consumer values – they're about as stable as a chocolate bar left in the sun. What was once seen as helpful information is now, for many, viewed as part of a problematic narrative around food, body image, and health.

Gatsby Chocolate, with its prominent calorie display, had inadvertently stepped into a generational and cultural shift. They'd created a product perfect for health-conscious consumers, only to find that the very definition of "health-conscious" was changing right under their feet.

Generational Shifts: From Diet Culture to Holistic Wellness

So, what's going on here? Why are younger generations giving the side-eye to something as seemingly innocuous as calorie counts?

The shift from diet culture to a more holistic view of wellness isn't just a trend – it's a fundamental reevaluation of how we think about health, food, and our bodies. For many Millennials and Gen Z'ers, the focus has moved from restriction and numbers to nourishment, enjoyment, and overall wellbeing.

This new paradigm values:

- Intuitive eating over strict calorie counting
- Body positivity and acceptance over an idealized body type
- Mental health as a crucial component of overall wellness
- Sustainability and ethical sourcing of ingredients
- Transparency in marketing and product claims

For a brand like Gatsby Chocolate, this shift presents both a challenge and an opportunity. The challenge lies in repositioning a product that was designed with the best intentions but might be perceived as out of touch. The opportunity? To lead the charge in creating truly mindful indulgences that align with these evolving values.

Values-Driven Design: Creating Products for Tomorrow's Consumers

So, how do we navigate this brave new world where consumer values are shifting faster than a chameleon on a disco floor? Here are some strategies to help you create products that don't just meet current needs but anticipate future values:

1. **Listen More Than You Speak**: Engage in ongoing dialogue with your target demographic. Use social media, focus groups, and surveys to really understand their values, concerns, and aspirations.
2. **Think Beyond the Product**: Consider the entire lifecycle of your product, from sourcing to disposal. How can you make each stage align with evolving ethical standards?
3. **Embrace Transparency**: Be open about your ingredients, processes, and the reasoning behind your design choices. Consumers appreciate brands that are willing to have honest conversations.
4. **Focus on Positive Messaging**: Instead of highlighting what your product lacks (e.g., low in calories), emphasize what it offers (e.g., made with high-quality, ethically sourced cocoa).
5. **Create an Inclusive Brand Narrative**: Ensure your marketing and packaging speak to a diverse audience and promote a positive relationship with food and health.
6. **Stay Agile**: Be prepared to pivot your messaging or even your product design as values continue to evolve. Flexibility is key in this rapidly changing landscape.

Exercise: Ethical Product Design Workshop

Ready to put these principles into action? Let's reimagine Gatsby Chocolate for the values-conscious consumer of tomorrow:

1. **Reframe the Value Proposition:**

- Current: "Low-calorie chocolate indulgence"
- Potential new angles: "Mindful moments of joy" or "Ethically crafted flavor experience"
2. **Redesign the Packaging:**
   - Remove prominent calorie display
   - Highlight ethical sourcing of ingredients
   - Incorporate messaging about balance and enjoyment
3. **Develop a Holistic Brand Story:**
   - Create a narrative that goes beyond nutrition facts
   - Emphasize the role of Gatsby Chocolate in a balanced lifestyle
   - Showcase the faces and stories behind the product (farmers, chocolatiers)
4. **Engage in Value-Aligned Partnerships:**
   - Collaborate with body positivity influencers
   - Partner with mental health organizations
   - Support cocoa farming communities
5. **Innovate Product Line:**
   - Develop limited edition flavors that celebrate cultural diversity
   - Create packaging options that are environmentally friendly
   - Offer a "choose your own adventure" product line where consumers can customize their chocolate experience

Remember, the goal isn't to jump on every trend that comes along. It's about deeply understanding the values that drive your consumers and creating products that resonate on a meaningful level.

In the end, Gatsby Chocolate's experience in the Shark Tank serves as a powerful reminder: in the world of product design and marketing, what you don't say can be just as important as what you do. By aligning with the evolving values of their target audience, brands like Gatsby have the opportunity to not just sell a product, but to become part of a larger conversation about health, happiness, and what it means to live well.

After all, in a world where consumer values are constantly shifting, the most successful brands won't just be the ones that create great products – they'll be the ones that create products that make consumers feel great about themselves, their choices, and their impact on the world.

Now that's a sweet success we can all feel good about indulging in.

The Gatsby Pitch 2.0: Reimagining the Shark Tank Moment

Before: The Original Pitch

Ryan and Doug stepped into the Shark Tank, introducing themselves as the brothers behind Halo Top ice cream. They presented Gatsby Chocolate as a healthier alternative to traditional chocolate, emphasizing its significantly reduced sugar and calorie content. Their pitch focused heavily on the nutritional aspects, with prominent display of calorie counts and comparisons to regular chocolate. They requested $500,000 for a 5% stake in their company, highlighting their distribution in major retailers like Walmart and Safeway.

After: The Reimagined Pitch

(The lights in the Shark Tank dim, and a soft, warm glow envelops the room. Ryan and Doug step forward, each holding an elegantly designed box of Gatsby Chocolate.)

Ryan: "Sharks, imagine a world where indulgence and mindfulness coexist in perfect harmony. A world where the joy of chocolate isn't overshadowed by guilt, but enhanced by purpose."

Doug: "We're Ryan and Doug, the minds behind Halo Top ice cream. But today, we're not here to talk about past successes. We're here to invite you on a new journey – one that's redefining the very essence of chocolate."

Ryan: "Introducing Gatsby Chocolate – a revolution in mindful indulgence."

(They open the boxes, revealing an array of beautifully crafted chocolate bars.)

Doug: "Now, you might be thinking, 'Not another health food pitch.' But Gatsby isn't just about health – it's about a holistic approach to pleasure and wellbeing."

Ryan: "We've created a chocolate that not only tastes incredible but aligns with the values of today's conscious consumers. Each bar is crafted with ethically sourced cocoa, supporting fair trade practices and sustainable farming."

Doug: "But here's where it gets interesting. We've managed to create a chocolate that has less sugar and fewer calories than traditional bars, without compromising on that rich, indulgent taste. And no, you won't find any glaring calorie counts on our packaging. Because Gatsby is about savoring the moment, not counting numbers."

Ryan: "We're in over 6,000 stores nationwide, including Walmart and Safeway. But here's the twist – we have national distribution without national awareness. And that's where you come in."

Doug: "We're not just looking for an investment; we're looking for partners who can help us bridge the gap between presence and recognition. We need your expertise to turn Gatsby from a product into a movement."

Ryan: "We're seeking $500,000 for a 5% stake in our company. But more than that, we're offering you the chance to be part of a brand that's redefining indulgence for a new generation."

Doug: "With Gatsby, we're not just selling chocolate. We're offering a moment of joy, a taste of luxury, and a choice that consumers can feel good about on every level."

Ryan: "So, Sharks, are you ready to join us in writing the next chapter of chocolate's rich history? Are you ready to prove that success can be both ethical and delicious?"

Doug: "The question isn't just whether you want to invest in Gatsby Chocolate. It's whether you want to be part of a movement that's making the world a little sweeter, one mindful bite at a time."

(Ryan and Doug stand confidently, offering the Sharks a taste of Gatsby Chocolate.)

Ryan and Doug (in unison): "So, Sharks, shall we indulge in success together?"

This reimagined pitch addresses the key lessons we've explored:

1. It embraces the "beginner's mind" by acknowledging past success but focusing on the new challenge at hand.
2. It directly addresses the awareness arbitrage issue, turning it into an opportunity for the Sharks.
3. It aligns with evolving consumer values, emphasizing ethical sourcing and a holistic approach to wellbeing rather than just calorie counts.

The new pitch positions Gatsby Chocolate not just as a product, but as a movement aligned with contemporary values and consumer desires. It invites the Sharks to be part of a larger narrative about changing the industry, rather than simply investing in a chocolate company.

Conclusion: The Future is Sweet (and Mindful)

As we wrap up our delectable journey through the world of Gatsby Chocolate, it's clear that this isn't just a story about a candy bar. It's a rich, multi-layered narrative about innovation, adaptability, and the ever-evolving landscape of consumer values. So, let's take a moment to savor the key lessons we've extracted from this entrepreneurial confection.

The Sweet Synthesis: Recapping Our Journey

1. **The Paradox of Past Success**: Ryan and Doug showed us that true innovation often requires us to unlearn our past triumphs. Their willingness to embrace a beginner's mind, even after the massive success of Halo Top, reminds us that in the world of entrepreneurship, your last win can be your biggest obstacle. The lesson? Don't let your past successes calcify into rigid thinking. Stay humble, stay hungry, and always be ready to start fresh.
2. **The Awareness Arbitrage**: Gatsby's predicament of having national distribution without national awareness highlighted a crucial truth of modern business: being everywhere isn't the same as being known. In a world cluttered with products and messages, bridging the gap between physical presence and mental real estate is the new frontier. The key is to craft a narrative that transcends your product, turning customers into advocates and shelf space into mind space.
3. **The Ethical Evolution**: The unexpected critique of Gatsby's calorie-focused packaging served as a poignant reminder that consumer values are constantly shifting. What was once a selling point can quickly become a liability. The future belongs to brands that can anticipate and align with evolving ethical standards, creating products that consumers can feel good about on every level – from personal health to global impact.

A Call to Sweetness: Embracing Change and Ethical Innovation

Now, my fellow entrepreneurs, as we stand at the crossroads of tradition and innovation, of profit and purpose, I challenge you to take these lessons to heart. The future of business isn't just about creating great products; it's about fostering great change.

1. **Cultivate Perpetual Curiosity**: Approach each new venture with the wide-eyed wonder of a beginner, regardless of your track record. Your next big idea might come from questioning the very foundations of your industry.
2. **Bridge the Awareness Gap**: Don't just focus on where your product is, but on how it lives in the minds and hearts of your consumers. Craft a story that turns customers into community.
3. **Lead with Values**: Anticipate the ethical considerations of tomorrow. Create products that not only serve a need but stand for something bigger. Remember, in the future, the most successful brands will be those that make consumers feel good about their choices.
4. **Embrace Adaptability**: The only constant in business is change. Build flexibility into your brand DNA, allowing you to pivot not just your strategies, but your entire ethos if necessary.
5. **Seek Meaningful Partnerships**: As Gatsby Chocolate sought in the Shark Tank, look for partners who bring more than just capital. Seek those who can amplify your vision and help navigate the complex terrain of modern business.

Remember, the entrepreneurs who will thrive in this new landscape aren't just innovators – they're ethical alchemists, turning the base metals of consumer needs into the gold of purposeful products. They're storytellers, crafting narratives that resonate deeply in a noisy world. They're futurists, anticipating the values of tomorrow and building them into the foundations of today's businesses.

So, as you embark on your own entrepreneurial adventures, ask yourself: Are you creating a product, or are you crafting an experience? Are you solving a problem, or are you contributing to a larger conversation? Are you building a business, or are you nurturing a movement?

The future is sweet, indeed – but it's also complex, mindful, and ripe with opportunity for those bold enough to redefine what success tastes like. So go forth, innovate with purpose, and remember – in the grand chocolate box of entrepreneurship, the most delightful surprises often come in unexpected flavors.

Now, who's ready to take a bite out of the future?

Bonus: The Gatsby Chocolate Challenge

Ready to put your entrepreneurial skills to the test? Welcome to the Gatsby Chocolate Challenge, where we'll take the lessons we've learned and apply them in practical, creative exercises. Strap in, future disruptors – it's time to turn theory into delicious reality!

A. "Rebrand It": Design a new packaging concept for Gatsby Chocolate

Objective: Create a packaging design that aligns with evolving consumer values while maintaining brand identity.

Exercise:

1. Sketch or describe a new packaging design for Gatsby Chocolate.
2. Explain how your design addresses the following:
    ○ Ethical sourcing and sustainability
    ○ Positive relationship with food (avoiding "diet culture" messaging)
    ○ Premium quality and indulgence
    ○ Brand story and values
3. Consider innovative materials or formats that could enhance the user experience.

Reflection Questions:

- How does your design communicate Gatsby's values without relying on calorie counts?
- In what ways does the packaging create a memorable unboxing experience?
- How might this new design influence consumer perceptions and purchasing decisions?

B. "Awareness Amplifier": Develop a viral marketing campaign idea

Objective: Create a campaign that bridges the gap between Gatsby's distribution and brand awareness.

Exercise:

1. Outline a viral marketing campaign for Gatsby Chocolate.
2. Include the following elements:
   - A catchy hashtag
   - A user-generated content component
   - A partnership with an unexpected brand or influencer
   - An offline element that drives online engagement
3. Describe how this campaign leverages current social media trends and platforms.

Reflection Questions:

- How does this campaign create emotional connections with potential customers?
- In what ways does it encourage sharing and community building?

- How might this campaign be adapted for different regional markets?

C. "Value Proposition Pivot": Reframe an existing product for changing consumer values

Objective: Reimagine an existing product to align with evolving ethical and wellness standards.

Exercise:

1. Choose a well-known product that might be seen as out of step with current values.
2. Reframe its value proposition to appeal to ethically-minded, wellness-focused consumers.
3. Outline changes to:
   - Product formulation (if applicable)
   - Marketing messaging
   - Brand partnerships or collaborations
   - Corporate social responsibility initiatives

Reflection Questions:

- How does this pivot change the product's target demographic?
- What potential challenges might arise from this reframing?
- How could this pivot influence the broader industry?

D. "Beginner's Blueprint": Create a 30-day plan to approach your business with fresh eyes

Objective: Develop a strategy to cultivate a "beginner's mind" and challenge assumptions in your business.

Exercise:

1. Create a 30-day plan with daily or weekly activities designed to help you see your business from new perspectives.
2. Include elements such as:
   - Reverse mentoring (learning from younger team members or interns)
   - Cross-departmental job shadowing
   - Customer immersion experiences
   - Competitive product use and analysis
   - Reading or courses outside your industry
3. Set specific goals for insights or ideas you hope to generate from this process.

Reflection Questions:

- How might this plan help you identify blind spots in your current strategy?
- In what ways could this exercise lead to innovative product or service ideas?
- How could you make "beginner's mind" a permanent part of your company culture?

Bonus Challenge: The Gatsby Gauntlet

For the truly ambitious, combine elements from all four challenges into one comprehensive project:

1. Rebrand Gatsby Chocolate with new packaging.
2. Create a viral campaign to launch the rebrand.
3. Pivot Gatsby's value proposition to align with a new, unexpected consumer trend.
4. Develop a 30-day plan for the Gatsby team to approach their relaunch with fresh eyes.

Present your Gatsby Gauntlet solution in a format of your choice (presentation, video, mock website, etc.) and share it on social media with the hashtag #GatsbyGauntlet. Who knows? You might just catch the eye of a real-world chocolate disruptor!

Remember, the goal of these challenges isn't just to come up with clever ideas – it's to stretch your entrepreneurial muscles, challenge your assumptions, and practice the art of ethical innovation. So don't be afraid to think big, get a little weird, and most importantly, have fun with it!

After all, in the world of entrepreneurship, sometimes the sweetest successes come from the most unexpected places. Now go forth and disrupt deliciously!

Pitch 2: Pie Wine

Pizza's New Wingman: The Pie Wine Revolution

In a lively and entertaining pitch, best friends Kevin Kline and Joshua Green from Los Angeles, California, stepped into the Shark Tank seeking $200,000 for 7.5% of their company, Pie Wine. With a blend of humor and passion, they introduced their product as the perfect pairing for one of America's favorite foods: pizza.

Product Name: Pie Wine

Pitch Summary: Kline and Green presented Pie Wine as a sweet, sparkling, easy-drinking canned table wine designed specifically to complement pizza. They positioned it as the "OG pizza wine" and "pizza's new side piece," aiming to reintroduce the concept of pairing pizza with a sweet, slightly bubbling wine inspired by Italian Lambrusco.

Founders: Kevin Kline and Joshua Green

Product Summary: Pie Wine offers three varieties of canned sparkling wine (Sweet Za, White Crisp, and World Famous Red) created to enhance the pizza-eating experience.

Category: Alcoholic Beverages / Wine

Deal Requested: $200,000 for 7.5% equity

Offer Made: No

Offer Terms: N/A

Deal Accepted: No

Deal Terms: N/A

Deal Sharks: None

Despite an engaging presentation and a promising start with distribution commitments in eight states, the Sharks ultimately decided not to invest. The founders' passion, personal investment, and early traction were acknowledged, but concerns about market saturation, competition, and the product's early stage led to all Sharks declining to make an offer. The pitch highlighted the challenges of entering a competitive market, even with a unique angle and strong personal commitment from the founders.

Uncorking the Truth: Why Pie Wine Didn't Pop in the Tank

Despite a charismatic pitch and a unique product concept, Pie Wine failed to secure an investment from the Sharks. Let's dissect the factors that influenced this outcome:

1. **Product Appeal and Branding:**
   - Positive: The Sharks enjoyed the taste and found the concept intriguing.
   - Negative: Some Sharks, like Mark Cuban, found the branding confusing and potentially detrimental.
2. **Market Potential and Competition:**
   - Positive: The founders demonstrated early traction with distribution commitments.
   - Negative: Sharks expressed concerns about market saturation and competition from big players.
3. **Founders' Background:**
   - Positive: The combination of Kevin's entertainment industry experience and Joshua's financial expertise was impressive.
   - Negative: The part-time nature of their involvement raised questions about commitment.
4. **Traction and Sales:**

- o Positive: Secured distribution in eight states within two weeks of launch.
- o Negative: No actual sales data or consumer feedback available due to the recent launch.

5. **Valuation and Investment:**
   - o Positive: The founders showed significant personal investment and commitment.
   - o Negative: The valuation seemed high for a company with no sales history.

6. **Timing and Market Readiness:**
   - o Positive: The product tapped into a growing trend in the alcoholic beverage market.
   - o Negative: The extremely early stage of the business made it risky for the Sharks.

Suggestions for Entrepreneurs:

1. **Clarity in Branding:** Ensure your packaging and messaging are clear and immediately understandable to consumers.
2. **Market Differentiation:** In saturated markets, clearly articulate your unique value proposition and how you stand out from competitors.
3. **Traction Matters:** Even if you're early-stage, try to gather some consumer feedback or initial sales data before seeking major investments.
4. **Full Commitment:** Be prepared to demonstrate full-time commitment to your venture, especially when seeking significant investment.
5. **Realistic Valuation:** Base your valuation on concrete metrics and be prepared to justify it, especially for early-stage companies.

6. **Timing is Key:** Consider the stage of your business when approaching investors. Sometimes, it's better to wait until you have more traction.
7. **Know Your Audience:** Research potential investors to ensure your product aligns with their portfolio and interests.
8. **Anticipate Concerns:** Prepare responses to potential objections about your market, competition, and business model.

By addressing these factors, entrepreneurs can increase their chances of success in high-stakes pitching situations like Shark Tank.

Vintage Wisdom: Three Profound Business Lessons from Pie Wine's Shark Tank Splash

Lesson 1. The Hyper-Niche Paradox: When Specificity Becomes a Double-Edged Sword

Business Lesson: Hyper-niche products can create strong brand identity but may limit market perception and investor appeal.

Scenario: Pie Wine positioned itself as the perfect pairing for pizza, creating a unique identity. While this specificity resonated with some Sharks, it also raised concerns about market limitations and investor fit.

Entrepreneurial Application: When developing a hyper-niche product, consider:

- The scalability beyond the initial niche
- How to communicate broader market potential without diluting the core concept
- Strategies to pivot or expand the product narrative if needed

Lesson 2. The Founder's Paradox: When Personal Investment Meets Investor Skepticism

Business Lesson: High personal investment can demonstrate commitment but may raise questions about business judgment and scalability.

Scenario: The founders' significant personal financial commitments, including selling a house and liquidating a 401(k), showed dedication but also sparked concerns about the business's ability to attract outside capital and scale sustainably.

Entrepreneurial Application: Balance personal investment with business acumen by:

- Articulating a clear path to profitability and return on investment
- Demonstrating strategic use of personal funds to achieve key milestones
- Showing how outside investment will catalyze growth beyond personal resources

Lesson 3. The Timing Tightrope: Navigating the Gap Between Concept and Proof

Business Lesson: There's a critical window between having a fully developed concept and demonstrating market proof that can make or break investment opportunities.

Scenario: Pie Wine had secured distribution deals but lacked sales data, placing them in a precarious position where their concept was proven but market acceptance wasn't.

Entrepreneurial Application: To successfully navigate this gap:

- Develop a staged investment strategy that aligns funding rounds with key proof points
- Create a compelling narrative that bridges current traction with future potential
- Consider alternative funding sources or strategic partnerships to build initial market proof

These lessons highlight the complex interplay between product conceptualization, market positioning, founder commitment, and timing in the entrepreneurial journey. By understanding and applying these insights, entrepreneurs can better prepare for the challenges of pitching to investors and positioning their products for success in competitive markets.

Introduction: When Pizza Met Its Match

Picture this: It's a Friday night, you're sprawled on the couch, a steaming box of pizza on the coffee table in front of you. Your hand reaches out, but instead of grasping a cold beer or fizzy soda, you wrap your fingers around... a chilled can of wine?

Welcome to the world of Pie Wine, where two enterprising friends dared to reimagine one of the most iconic food pairings in American culture. It's a tale that would make even the most stoic of philosophers raise an eyebrow – and perhaps reach for a slice.

The Unexpected Pairing: Pizza and Wine Reimagined

For decades, the go-to beverage for pizza night has been beer or soda. It's a pairing as American as, well, pizza itself (despite its Italian origins). But Kevin Kline and Joshua Green, two lifelong friends from Los Angeles, looked at this established norm and asked, "What if?"

What if, instead of the usual suspects, we paired our pepperoni with a perfectly crafted wine? Not just any wine, mind you, but a sweet, sparkling concoction that complements the savory, cheesy goodness of a pizza slice. A wine that doesn't demand a corkscrew or a fancy glass – just a cold can and a willing palate.

This isn't just about slapping some wine in a can and calling it a day. No, Kline and Green's vision for Pie Wine was nothing short of revolutionary in its simplicity. They aimed to recreate the experience of Italian Lambrusco – a slightly sparkling, often sweet red wine that Italians have been enjoying with their pizza for generations – and make it accessible to the average American consumer.

It's the kind of idea that makes you wonder why nobody thought of it before. Or perhaps more accurately, why nobody had the audacity to challenge the status quo so directly. It's a reminder that innovation often lies not in inventing something entirely new, but in reimagining the familiar in unfamiliar ways.

Setting the Stage: Kevin and Joshua's Journey to the Tank

Now, let's talk about the masterminds behind this vinous revolution. Kevin Kline and Joshua Green aren't just business partners; they're best friends with a friendship spanning over three decades. Their journey to the Shark Tank is a testament to the power of long-standing relationships and shared dreams.

Kevin, a seasoned radio host with 20 years of experience entertaining the masses on KROQ in Los Angeles, brings the "fun" to the business. He's the guy who proposed to his wife with a ring hidden in a cupcake – a move that speaks volumes about his flair for the unexpected and his understanding of memorable experiences.

On the other hand, Joshua is the numbers guy. With a law degree, a master's in accounting, and a background in investment banking, he's the steady hand on the financial tiller. Currently serving as CFO of a major spatial computing video game company, Joshua brings a level of business acumen that complements Kevin's creative energy.

Their journey wasn't just about creating a product; it was about taking a leap of faith together. Joshua liquidated his 401(k), while Kevin and his wife sold their house to fund this venture. It's the kind of all-in move that would make a Vegas high-roller pause.

Walking into the Shark Tank, these two friends weren't just pitching a product; they were presenting a dream, a friendship, and a willingness to risk it all on a shared vision. It's the stuff great entrepreneurial stories are made of – whether they succeed or fail, they're all in, together.

Three Game-Changing Lessons for Niche Product Entrepreneurs

Now, you might be thinking, "Great story, but what's in it for me?" Well, buckle up, aspiring entrepreneur, because the Pie Wine Shark Tank experience is about to uncork some vintage wisdom that applies far beyond the world of pizza and wine.

As we dive deeper into this tale, we'll explore three game-changing lessons that every niche product entrepreneur needs to hear:

1. **The Hyper-Niche Paradox**: We'll uncover the power and pitfalls of carving out a super-specific market niche. How narrow is too narrow? When does specialization become limitation?
2. **The Founder's Paradox**: We'll examine the double-edged sword of personal investment. At what point does "skin in the game" become a red flag for potential investors?
3. **The Timing Tightrope**: We'll navigate the precarious balance between having a fully baked concept and proving market acceptance. How do you convince investors when you're caught in the no-man's land between idea and proven success?

These lessons, distilled from the Pie Wine pitch, offer a potent blend of insight that can help you navigate the often turbulent waters of entrepreneurship. Whether you're dreaming up the next big thing in your garage or preparing for your own Shark Tank moment, these insights will give you food for thought – and maybe even a new perspective on what to drink with your next slice of pizza.

So, grab a seat at the table (or couch – we don't judge), maybe even pop open a cold one (be it beer, soda, or yes, even canned wine), and let's dive into the rich, sometimes bubbly, always enlightening world of niche product entrepreneurship. After all, in the words of the ancient Stoic philosopher Seneca, "Luck is what happens when preparation meets opportunity." And who knows? Your next big idea might be hiding in the most unexpected of pairings.

Lesson 1: The Hyper-Niche Gambit: Slicing the Market Pie

Imagine walking into a party where everyone's talking about the same thing, but you're the only one with something genuinely new to say. That's the power of a hyper-niche product. It's not just about being different; it's about being the only one in the room who truly gets it. This is the world Pie Wine stepped into when they decided to become pizza's new best friend.

Defining the Pizza-Wine Connection

Let's face it, pizza and beer have been in a long-term relationship for decades. It's comfortable, it's familiar, and let's be honest, it's a bit boring. Enter Pie Wine, the daring homewrecker of the food pairing world. Kevin and Joshua didn't just create a new wine; they resurrected an old Italian tradition and gave it a modern, American twist.

Think about it. When's the last time you saw a beverage that was explicitly designed to go with a specific food? Sure, we have wine pairings, but those are suggestions, not dedicated products. Pie Wine took a leap and said, "We're not just good with pizza; we're made for pizza." It's like they looked at the entire beverage industry and decided to color outside the lines – with pizza sauce.

The Power and Pitfalls of Hyper-Niche Marketing

Now, let's talk about the double-edged sword that is hyper-niche marketing. On one side, you have the power of specificity. Pie Wine isn't trying to be everything to everyone. They're not competing with every wine on the shelf or trying to muscle in on beer's territory. They've carved out their own little corner of the market, and in that corner, they reign supreme.

This level of focus allows for laser-targeted marketing. Every ad, every piece of packaging, every social media post can be tailored to resonate with pizza lovers. It's not about convincing people to like wine; it's about convincing pizza enthusiasts that their favorite food has been missing its soulmate all along.

But here's where it gets tricky. The very specificity that gives Pie Wine its strength can also be its Achilles' heel. What happens when people want to drink it with something other than pizza? Or worse, what if they don't eat pizza at all? It's a bit like being the world's best penguin trainer – impressive, but with a somewhat limited market.

This is the tightrope that hyper-niche products have to walk. How do you stay true to your core identity while not painting yourself into a corner? It's a challenge that requires constant innovation and a deep understanding of your market.

"Expanding Your Slice"

Strategies for Broadening Appeal Without Losing Core Identity

1. **The Companion Strategy**: Instead of broadening the product itself, expand the range of companions. Pie Wine could start suggesting pairings with other Italian foods, positioning itself as the go-to drink for all things Mediterranean.
2. **The Occasion Expansion**: Move beyond the food pairing and focus on the occasion. Pie Wine could market itself as the perfect drink for movie nights, game days, or casual get-togethers – all occasions where pizza often makes an appearance.
3. **The Product Line Extension**: Develop new products that maintain the core identity but appeal to different tastes. Think "Pie Wine Light" for calorie-conscious consumers or "Spicy Pie Wine" for those who like their pizza with an extra kick.
4. **The Cultural Bridge**: Leverage the Italian connection to position Pie Wine as a cultural experience, not just a beverage. It's not just wine; it's a taste of the Italian lifestyle.
5. **The Collaboration Game**: Partner with pizza chains, Italian restaurants, or even non-food brands that align with the casual, fun vibe of pizza nights. This expands reach without diluting the core message.

Action Plan: Crafting a Scalable Niche Product Narrative

1. **Define Your Core**: Write down the three non-negotiable aspects of your product's identity. For Pie Wine, it might be "sparkling," "sweet," and "pizza-friendly."
2. **Identify Adjacencies**: List five related areas where your product could naturally expand. Think related foods, occasions, or cultural connections.
3. **Create Expansion Scenarios**: Develop three potential storylines for how your product could grow without losing its essence. For example, "From Pizza Parties to Mediterranean Nights: The Pie Wine Journey."
4. **Test the Boundaries**: Conduct small-scale experiments with your target audience to see how far you can push the product concept without losing their interest.
5. **Craft Your Evolution Story**: Write a brand narrative that shows how your product can grow and adapt while staying true to its roots. This becomes your roadmap and your pitch to investors and consumers alike.

Remember, the goal isn't to be everything to everyone. It's about finding that sweet spot where you're specific enough to be special, but flexible enough to grow. In the end, Pie Wine's success won't just be about how well it pairs with pizza, but how well it can pair its core identity with the changing tastes of the market.

So, the next time you're crafting your own niche product, ask yourself: Are you just serving a slice, or are you expanding the whole pie?

Lesson 2: The All-In Entrepreneur: Betting the House (Literally)

Picture this: You're standing at the edge of a cliff, looking down at the churning waters of entrepreneurship below. In one hand, you're clutching your life savings, and in the other, the deed to your house. The wind of opportunity is at your back, and you're faced with a choice: step back to safety or take the plunge. For Kevin Kline and Joshua Green of Pie Wine, the choice was clear – they jumped, house and all.

Skin in the Game: When Founders Go All-In

There's a certain romance to the idea of the all-in entrepreneur, isn't there? It's the stuff of Silicon Valley legends – the garage startups, the maxed-out credit cards, the sleeping bags under desks. But when Kevin casually mentioned selling his house to fund Pie Wine, he wasn't just sharing a financial decision; he was giving us a master class in commitment.

This level of personal investment goes beyond mere funding. It's a statement to the world, and more importantly, to yourself. It says, "I believe in this so much, I'm willing to risk everything." It's the entrepreneurial equivalent of burning the ships upon reaching the new world – there's no going back.

But here's the kicker: in the world of startups, this kind of all-in mentality isn't just admired; it's often expected. Investors want to see that you have skin in the game. They want to know that you're not just playing with their money, but that you're right there in the trenches, fighting with everything you've got.

The Double-Edged Sword of Personal Investment

Now, let's talk about the elephant in the room – or should I say, the sold house in the subdivision. Going all-in like Kevin and Joshua did is a double-edged sword, and both edges are sharp enough to draw blood.

On one side, you have the undeniable power of commitment. When you've put everything on the line, failure isn't just disappointing; it's existentially threatening. This kind of pressure can be a powerful motivator, pushing you to work harder, think smarter, and persevere through challenges that might otherwise break you.

Moreover, this level of personal investment can be incredibly attractive to potential partners and investors. It shows a level of confidence and dedication that's hard to fake. After all, if you're willing to bet your house on this idea, it must be pretty damn good, right?

But here's where it gets tricky. The other edge of that sword is just as sharp, and it's called desperation. When you've gone all-in, the lines between passionate and reckless can blur. You might find yourself making decisions based on fear rather than strategy, clinging to sunk costs rather than adapting to market realities.

There's also the question of sustainability. Sure, selling your house might give you a nice chunk of capital to start with, but what happens when that runs out? Without a safety net, every setback becomes a potential catastrophe.

And let's not forget the human cost. The stress of having everything on the line can be overwhelming, affecting not just you but your relationships, your health, and your ability to make clear-headed decisions.

"Balancing Passion and Pragmatism"

Tactics for Demonstrating Commitment Without Raising Red Flags

1. **The Staged Investment Approach**: Instead of going all-in at once, create a roadmap of personal investments tied to specific business milestones. This shows commitment while maintaining a safety net.
2. **The Skills Investment**: Demonstrate your commitment by investing heavily in developing new skills crucial to your business. This could mean taking courses, attending workshops, or even working for free in related industries to gain experience.
3. **The Time Over Money Strategy**: If you can't invest huge sums, invest your time. Document the hours you're putting in, especially if you're working on your startup alongside a day job.

This kind of "sweat equity" can be just as impressive as financial investment.

4. **The Strategic Sacrifice**: Instead of selling your house, make calculated sacrifices that directly benefit your business. This could mean downsizing to a smaller apartment and using the saved rent for business expenses, or selling a car to buy necessary equipment.

5. **The Partial Liquidity Play**: Rather than liquidating all your assets, consider options like home equity loans or selling a portion of your investments. This shows commitment while maintaining some financial stability.

Checklist: Smart Personal Investment Strategies for Startups

1. Set a Personal Investment Cap: Decide on a maximum percentage of your net worth you're willing to invest. This ensures you're committed but not reckless.

2. Create a Runway Budget: Calculate how long your personal investment will sustain the business and have a plan for what happens after.

3. Maintain Emergency Reserves: Keep at least 3-6 months of living expenses in a separate, untouchable account.

4. Diversify Your Personal Investment: Don't put all your eggs in one basket. Spread your investment across different aspects of the business.

5. Set Clear Milestones: Tie additional personal investments to specific business achievements to ensure you're not throwing good money after bad.

6. Explore Alternative Funding: Look into grants, competitions, or accelerator programs that could provide funding without additional personal risk.
7. Regular Reality Checks: Schedule monthly or quarterly reviews to assess whether your personal investment is paying off and adjust accordingly.
8. Exit Strategy: Have a clear plan for what happens if things don't work out. Know your 'uncle point' in advance.

Remember, being an all-in entrepreneur doesn't mean being a reckless one. The goal is to demonstrate unwavering commitment to your vision while maintaining the pragmatism necessary for long-term success. It's about betting the house on your idea – but making sure you've got somewhere to sleep at night.

So, as you stand on that entrepreneurial cliff, ready to take the plunge, ask yourself: Are you jumping in with passion and a plan, or are you just falling with style?

Lesson 3: The Timing Tango: Dancing Between Concept and Proof

Picture yourself on a dance floor. The music's just started, and you're poised to make your move. But here's the catch – you're dancing solo, and you need a partner to really shine. That partner? It's called market validation, and timing your steps with it is the difference between a show-stopping performance and stumbling off the floor. Welcome to the Timing Tango, where entrepreneurs like Kevin and Joshua from Pie Wine learn to dance between the beats of concept and proof.

The Critical Window of Investment Opportunity

In the world of startups, timing isn't just important – it's everything. There's a sweet spot, a Goldilocks zone if you will, where your idea is developed enough to be compelling, but early enough that investors can still get in on the ground floor. Miss this window, and you might find yourself either too early (hello, skepticism) or too late (sorry, the party's already over).

Pie Wine found themselves smack in the middle of this critical window when they stepped into the Shark Tank. They had more than just an idea – they had a product, packaging, and even distribution deals. But here's where it gets interesting: they didn't have sales data.

They were dancing right on the edge of concept and proof, trying to convince the Sharks to join them before the music changed.

This is the entrepreneur's dilemma. Go too early, and you risk being dismissed as a dreamer with a half-baked idea. Wait too long, and you might miss out on the capital you need to scale. It's like trying to catch a wave – paddle too soon, and you'll exhaust yourself before the wave arrives; too late, and you'll be left bobbing in the wake.

Navigating the No-Man's Land Between Idea and Market Validation

So, how do you navigate this treacherous territory? It's all about building bridges as you cross them. Pie Wine did this by securing distribution deals before they had sales. It's a brilliant move – it shows potential without requiring actual market performance. It's like having a dance card filled out before the ball even starts.

But here's the rub – potential isn't performance. The Sharks' hesitation stemmed from this very gap. Sure, Pie Wine had distributors excited, but would consumers bite? This is the no-man's land every startup must cross – the space between "great idea" and "proven concept."

Navigating this space requires a delicate balance of confidence and humility. You need to be bold enough to ask for investment based on potential, but humble enough to acknowledge the risks. It's about painting a vision of the future while standing firmly in the present.

"Bridging the Proof Gap"

Techniques for Building Credibility in Early-Stage Ventures

1. **The Micro-Test Gambit**: Before going big, go small. Run limited releases or pop-up events to gather real-world data. It's like a dress rehearsal before opening night.
2. **The Expert Endorsement Play**: Get industry leaders or influencers to vouch for your concept. It's social proof before market proof.
3. **The Parallel Proof Strategy**: If you can't prove your exact concept, prove components of it. Show success in related areas that support your main idea.
4. **The Pre-Order Push**: Generate excitement and validation through pre-orders. It's not just potential interest; it's potential customers putting their money where their mouth is.
5. **The Pilot Program Approach**: Partner with a few key customers or businesses for a pilot run. It's a controlled environment to demonstrate real-world application.
6. **The Data-Driven Hypothesis**: Use market research and data analytics to build a compelling case for your product's potential success. It's not proof, but it's the next best thing.
7. **The Incremental Launch Method**: Instead of an all-or-nothing approach, launch features or products incrementally, using each small success to build credibility for the larger vision.

Exercise: Mapping Your Proof-of-Concept Timeline

1. **Current State Assessment:**
   - List your current assets (product development stage, partnerships, etc.)
   - Identify your biggest credibility gaps
2. **Milestone Mapping:**
   - Plot key milestones on a timeline (product completion, first sale, break-even point)
   - Identify the "proof points" that would significantly boost your credibility at each stage
3. **Resource Allocation:**
   - For each milestone, list the resources needed (time, money, skills)
   - Identify which resources you have and which you need to acquire
4. **Risk Assessment:**
   - For each stage, identify potential risks or roadblocks
   - Develop contingency plans for major risks
5. **Credibility Boosters:**
   - For each stage, list actions you can take to boost credibility (e.g., securing a key partnership, getting media coverage)
   - Prioritize these actions based on impact and feasibility
6. **Investment Staging:**
   - Identify optimal points for seeking different levels of investment
   - Align these points with your proof-of-concept milestones

7. **Narrative Development:**
   - Craft a compelling story that links your current state to your end goal
   - Highlight how each milestone brings you closer to market validation
8. **Review and Adjust:**
   - Set regular intervals to review and adjust your timeline
   - Be prepared to pivot based on new information or changing market conditions

Remember, the goal of this exercise isn't to predict the future with certainty. It's to create a roadmap that demonstrates your understanding of the journey from concept to proof, and shows potential investors that you have a plan to bridge that gap.

In the end, the Timing Tango isn't about perfect steps – it's about keeping rhythm with the changing beat of the market. It's about being prepared to twirl when opportunity presents itself, and to dip when challenges arise. So as you map out your own proof-of-concept timeline, ask yourself: Are you ready to lead this dance, or are you just following someone else's steps?

For Pie Wine, their dance in the Shark Tank might not have ended with an investment, but it certainly wasn't their last waltz. Every startup's journey is a long and winding choreography of concept, proof, and persistence. So put on your dancing shoes, entrepreneurs. The music's playing, and it's time to show the market your best moves.

Reimagining the Pitch: Pie Wine 2.0

Before: The Original Shark Tank Presentation

Kevin and Joshua entered the Tank with enthusiasm, introducing Pie Wine as a sweet, sparkling, easy-drinking canned wine designed specifically for pizza. They requested $200,000 for 7.5% equity, emphasizing their product as "the OG pizza wine" and "pizza's new side piece." Their pitch highlighted the Italian tradition of pairing sweet, bubbly wine with pizza, and they showcased three varieties of their product.

The founders mentioned their recent launch, distribution in eight states, and commitments from distributors worth $300,000 to $400,000. They shared their backgrounds - Kevin as a radio host and Joshua as a CFO with investment banking experience. They also revealed significant personal investments, including selling a house and liquidating a 401(k).

While the Sharks enjoyed the taste, they expressed concerns about market saturation, unclear branding, and the early stage of the business. Despite the founders' passion and early traction, all Sharks ultimately declined to invest.

After: A Refined Pitch Incorporating Key Lessons

[Kevin and Joshua enter, each holding a can of Pie Wine and a slice of pizza]

Kevin: "Sharks, imagine transforming an everyday moment into an unforgettable experience. That's exactly what we're doing with Pie Wine."

Joshua: "We're Joshua Green and Kevin Kline, and we're here to introduce you to the next revolution in the $46 billion US pizza market. We're seeking $200,000 for 5% of Pie Wine, the first beverage engineered specifically to enhance your pizza experience."

Kevin: "Now, you might be thinking, 'Pizza already has a drink - beer.' But here's where it gets interesting. We're not competing with beer; we're creating an entirely new category: experience-enhancing beverages."

Joshua: "Pie Wine isn't just a drink. It's a sensory symphony designed to elevate your pizza night. Our proprietary blend of sweetness and bubbles doesn't just complement pizza - it transforms it. It's like upgrading from standard definition to 4K for your taste buds."

Kevin: "We've taken a forgotten Italian tradition and reimagined it for the modern American palate. It's innovation rooted in nostalgia, familiarity with a twist."

Joshua: "In just two months since launch, we've secured distribution in eight states, with commitments from distributors worth over $400,000. But that's just the beginning. We're not just selling wine; we're selling the ultimate pizza night experience."

Kevin: "We've identified three key growth strategies:

1. The Companion Expansion: Moving beyond pizza to all Italian cuisine.
2. The Occasion Domination: Becoming the go-to drink for all casual dining experiences.
3. The Cultural Bridge: Positioning Pie Wine as a taste of the Italian lifestyle, accessible to all."

Joshua: "We're not just founders; we're our own best case study in commitment. We've invested over $300,000 of our own money, including liquidating our 401(k)s and selling a house. But we're not doing this recklessly. We have a clear roadmap to profitability and a strategy to make Pie Wine a household name."

Kevin: "To prove our concept, we've partnered with three local pizzerias for a pilot program. In just one month, they've reported a 15% increase in beverage sales when offering Pie Wine. We're not just claiming potential; we're showing real-world results."

Joshua: "Pie Wine isn't just a product; it's a movement. We're not asking you to invest in a beverage; we're inviting you to join us in redefining how America enjoys its favorite food. Who's ready to take a bite out of this opportunity and help us turn every pizza night into a Pie Wine night?"

Analysis: Breaking Down the Improvements

1. **Sensory Synergy Focus**: The revised pitch emphasizes Pie Wine as an experience

enhancer, not just a beverage. This addresses the "Taste-Tuning" lesson, positioning the product as a lifestyle enhancer rather than just a drink.

2. **Market Creation Angle**: By framing Pie Wine as creating a new category of "experience-enhancing beverages," the pitch sidesteps direct competition with established drinks like beer. This aligns with the "Scenario Supremacy" lesson, focusing on dominating a specific consumer scenario.

3. **Nostalgia Alchemy**: The pitch now explicitly mentions the blend of innovation and tradition, leveraging the "Retro-vation" concept to give the product both novelty and familiarity.

4. **Growth Strategy Clarity**: The presentation outlines clear strategies for expanding beyond the initial pizza pairing, addressing potential concerns about limited market appeal.

5. **Staged Commitment**: While still highlighting their personal investment, the founders now present it as part of a strategic plan rather than an all-or-nothing gamble. This demonstrates commitment while suggesting a more measured approach to risk.

6. **Proof of Concept**: The addition of the pilot program results provides tangible evidence of market potential, bridging the gap between concept and proof that was missing in the original pitch.

7. **Visionary Appeal**: The pitch now frames Pie Wine as a movement and invites the Sharks to be part of redefining a cultural experience, appealing to their desire to be part of something bigger than just another product.

8. **Valuation Adjustment:** By asking for the same amount for a smaller equity stake, the founders demonstrate confidence in their product's value while still offering an attractive opportunity for the Sharks.

This reimagined pitch addresses the key weaknesses of the original presentation while leveraging the unique strengths of Pie Wine. It presents a more strategic, market-aware approach that could potentially resonate more strongly with investors looking for innovative, high-growth opportunities.

Conclusion: Savoring the Lessons, Preparing for Success

As we uncork the final thoughts on Pie Wine's Shark Tank journey, it's clear that their experience offers far more than just a tale of a pizza-paired beverage. It's a rich vintage of entrepreneurial insights, aged in the oak barrels of real-world challenges and opportunities. Let's take a moment to savor these lessons one last time, and see how their flavors can enhance the palate of entrepreneurs across all industries.

Recap of Key Insights from Pie Wine's Shark Tank Experience

1. **The Art of Sensory Synergy**: Pie Wine showed us that true innovation isn't just about creating a new product; it's about orchestrating a multidimensional experience. They didn't just make wine; they crafted a companion to elevate an everyday moment into something special.
2. **The Power of Hyper-Niche Focus**: By zeroing in on the specific scenario of pizza consumption, Pie Wine demonstrated the potential of dominating micro-moments in consumer life. This laser focus allowed them to sidestep competition from broader market players and carve out their own unique space.
3. **The Delicate Balance of All-In Commitment**: Kevin and Joshua's willingness to bet big on

their idea - even selling a house to fund it - highlighted both the power and the pitfalls of going all-in. Their story reminds us that while passion is crucial, it must be tempered with pragmatism to be truly effective.

4. **The Timing Tango of Concept and Proof**: Pie Wine's pitch illustrated the critical dance between having a compelling concept and providing market validation. Their journey underscores the importance of building credibility bridges as you move from idea to proven success.

5. **The Alchemy of Nostalgia and Innovation**: By reimagining an Italian tradition for the modern American market, Pie Wine showed how mining collective memory can lead to innovations that feel both novel and familiar.

The Bigger Picture: Applying These Lessons Across Industries

While Pie Wine's story is unique, the lessons it offers are universally applicable:

1. **Experience is the New Product**: Regardless of your industry, consider how you can transform your offering from a mere product or service into a comprehensive experience. Whether you're selling software or sandwiches, there's always an opportunity to orchestrate a sensory symphony.

2. **Micro-Moments Matter**: Look for underserved scenarios in your industry. Dominating a hyper-

specific niche can be more valuable than being a small fish in a big, general market.

3. **Strategic All-In:** Passion and commitment are vital, but they must be channeled strategically. Create a roadmap for your all-in moments, ensuring that your big bets are calculated and sustainable.

4. **Prove as You Move:** Build validation into your development process. Look for ways to gather real-world data and feedback at every stage, creating a continuum of proof rather than a binary state of unproven or proven.

5. **Bridge Past and Future:** Look to history, tradition, and cultural memory for inspiration. The next big innovation might be hiding in plain sight, waiting for someone to give it a modern twist.

Call to Action: Embracing the Entrepreneur's Journey, Setbacks and All

As we close this chapter on Pie Wine's Shark Tank adventure, remember that their story didn't end in the Tank. Every "no" is just a "not yet," and every setback is a setup for a comeback.

To all the entrepreneurs out there, whether you're pairing wine with pizza or disrupting an entirely different industry, here's your call to action:

1. **Embrace the Journey**: Understand that the path of entrepreneurship is rarely a straight line. Embrace the twists, turns, and occasional U-turns as part of the adventure.
2. **Seek Synergy**: Look for unexpected combinations in your industry. Your pizza and wine moment is out there - find it, refine it, and serve it to the world.
3. **Dance with Timing**: Don't wait for perfect conditions. Start your timing tango now, and adjust your steps as you go.
4. **Commit Smartly**: Go all-in on your dream, but do it with a strategy. Let your passion fuel you, but let wisdom guide you.
5. **Learn from Every Pitch**: Whether you get a "yes," a "no," or a "maybe," there's always a lesson to be learned. Extract the insights, refine your approach, and keep moving forward.

Remember, in the world of entrepreneurship, every day is a new opportunity to uncork your potential. Your idea might just be the next big thing that nobody knew they needed. So raise a glass (of Pie Wine or whatever inspires you) to the journey ahead.

Here's to the dreamers, the risk-takers, and the innovators. May your ventures be bold, your strategies be sound, and your success be sweet and bubbly.

Now, go out there and make your mark. The entrepreneurial world is your pizza, and you've got the perfect wine to pair with it. Salute!

Entrepreneurs' Tasting Menu: Interactive Exercises

Get ready to roll up your sleeves and put your entrepreneurial skills to the test. These exercises are designed to help you apply the lessons from Pie Wine's Shark Tank experience to your own venture. Grab a notebook, pour yourself a glass of creativity, and let's begin!

1. "Niche Expansion Workshop": Broadening Your Product's Appeal

Objective: Develop strategies to expand your niche product's appeal without losing its core identity.

Exercise:

1. Write down your product's core purpose and target audience.
2. List 5 adjacent markets or user groups that could benefit from your product.
3. For each new market, brainstorm 3 minor modifications to your product that could make it more appealing.
4. Create a "product expansion map" showing your core product in the center, with branches to each new market and the associated modifications.
5. Evaluate each branch for feasibility and potential impact. Rank them in order of priority.

6. Write a brief (2-3 sentence) pitch for your top-ranked expansion idea.

Reflection: How can you maintain your product's unique identity while appealing to a broader audience? What risks might come with expansion, and how can you mitigate them?

2. "The Investor's Palate": Aligning Personal Passion with Investor Expectations

Objective: Learn to present your personal commitment in a way that resonates with investors without raising red flags.

Exercise:

1. List 5 ways you've personally invested in your business (time, money, skills, etc.).
2. For each investment, write down: a) The potential benefit to the business b) The personal risk involved c) How it demonstrates your commitment
3. Now, put on an "investor hat." For each item, rate on a scale of 1-5: a) How impressive this commitment would be to an investor b) How concerning this level of risk might be to an investor
4. Based on these ratings, craft a 30-second speech about your commitment that highlights the most impressive aspects while addressing potential concerns.

5. Practice delivering this speech to a friend or mentor and ask for feedback.

Reflection: How can you demonstrate deep commitment to your venture while also showing that you're a prudent risk-taker? What's the right balance between passion and pragmatism in your pitch?

3. "Timing Your Vintage": Plotting the Perfect Moment to Seek Investment

Objective: Develop a timeline for your venture that identifies optimal points for seeking investment.

Exercise:

1. Create a timeline of your venture from idea conception to full market validation. Mark where you are now.
2. Identify 5 key milestones on this journey (e.g., prototype completion, first sale, break-even point).
3. For each milestone, list: a) Resources needed to reach it b) Proof of concept it provides c) Potential risks or challenges
4. Now, mark 3 potential "investment zones" on your timeline where seeking funding could be most beneficial.
5. For each zone, write a brief pitch explaining why that would be the right time for an investor to get involved.
6. Finally, create a "preparation checklist" for each investment zone, listing what you need to have

ready to make the most compelling case to investors.

Reflection: How does the timing of investment affect your venture's potential and risk profile? How can you build your business to create the most attractive investment opportunities?

4. "Pairing Perfection": Matching Your Product to the Right Investors

Objective: Learn to identify and appeal to the most suitable investors for your unique venture.

Exercise:

1. List 5 key features or aspects of your product/business.
2. For each feature, brainstorm a type of investor who might find it particularly appealing (e.g., tech enthusiasts, sustainability advocates, market disruptors).
3. Research and list 3 real investors or investment firms that fit each investor type you identified.
4. For each investor/firm, note: a) Their typical investment size and stage b) Recent investments they've made c) Any public statements about what they look for in investments
5. Based on this research, craft a unique one-paragraph pitch for each investor type, highlighting the aspects of your business that would most appeal to them.

6. Finally, create a "perfect investor" profile, combining the most desirable traits for your specific venture.

Reflection: How does understanding investor preferences change your approach to pitching? How can you position your product to appeal to the right investors without compromising your vision?

Remember, like pairing the perfect wine with a dish, finding the right match between your venture and potential investors is an art. It requires understanding both your own "flavors" and the "palate" of your audience. Use these exercises to refine your entrepreneurial recipe and prepare for your next big pitch.

Cheers to your success, and may your venture be as perfectly paired as pizza and Pie Wine!

Pitch 3: Gently Soap

Botanical Bliss: Gently Soap's Sensitive Skin Revolution

In a heartfelt pitch that blended personal struggle with entrepreneurial spirit, Kristen Dunning stepped into the Shark Tank seeking a $75,000 investment for a 10% equity stake in her company, Gently Soap. Born from her lifelong battle with eczema and rooted in her family's agricultural legacy, Gently Soap offers a line of bath products that eliminates essential oils and synthetic fragrances while maintaining a gentle, natural aroma.

Product Name: Gently Soap

Founder: Kristen Dunning

Product Summary: A line of all-natural, botanical soap bars designed for people with sensitive skin, eczema, and psoriasis. The soaps use proprietary herbal infusions instead of essential oils or synthetic fragrances.

Category: Personal Care / Beauty

Deal Requested: $75,000 for 10% equity

Offer Made: Yes

Offer Terms: $75,000 for 25% equity

Deal Accepted: Yes

Deal Terms: $75,000 for 25% equity

Deal Shark: Candace Nelson

Kristen's pitch was a masterclass in turning personal adversity into business opportunity. She shared her touching story of childhood eczema, which led to hair loss and bullying, fueling her determination to create a solution. Her background in agricultural research and horticulture, inspired by her grandparents' 84-acre farm, gave her the expertise to develop Gently Soap's unique formulations.

The Sharks were impressed by Gently Soap's financials: $113,000 in total sales since February 2021, with $66,000 in the previous year alone, yielding a profit of $38,000. The company's 78% repeat customer rate and low customer acquisition cost of $5.83 further piqued their interest.

While Mark Cuban, Daymond John, and Barbara Corcoran opted out, Kevin O'Leary saw potential in the high margins and offered a royalty deal. However, it was Candace Nelson who connected most deeply with Kristen's passion-driven approach. After some negotiation, Kristen accepted Candace's offer of $75,000 for 25% equity, securing not just an investment but a partner who believed in her vision of bringing joy and relief to those with sensitive skin.

From Skin Irritation to Market Sensation: Gently Soap's Winning Formula

Kristen Dunning's Gently Soap didn't just clean up in the Tank; it revealed a blueprint for turning personal pain into entrepreneurial gain. Let's break down the elements that made the Sharks sit up and take notice:

1. **Personal Pain Point to Market Opportunity:** Kristen's lifelong struggle with eczema wasn't just a sob story; it was market research in disguise. By solving her own problem, she tapped into a growing segment - 71% of the population with sensitive skin, up from 55% in two decades.
2. **Roots That Run Deep:** Her agricultural background and family legacy weren't just backstory fluff. They provided the expertise and authenticity that set Gently Soap apart in a crowded market.
3. **Numbers That Sparkle:** With $113,000 in total sales, a 78% repeat customer rate, and a customer acquisition cost of just $5.83, Gently Soap proved it wasn't just a feel-good story - it was a viable business.
4. **Margins That Make Waves:** At $2.38 production cost for an $11 retail price, Gently Soap's margins were clean enough to make even Mr. Wonderful salivate.
5. **A Product You Can See (and Smell):** The Sharks could literally see the herbs and flowers in the soap, providing tangible proof of the product's natural claims.

6. **Passion Meets Professionalism:** Kristen's emotional connection to her product was balanced by her MBA-level grasp of her financials and market position.
7. **Untapped Potential:** With plans to launch on Amazon and room for retail expansion, Gently Soap showed it was just getting started.
8. **A Story Worth Telling:** In Candace Nelson, Kristen found a Shark who saw beyond the numbers to the narrative potential of the brand.

For aspiring entrepreneurs, Gently Soap's success offers some key takeaways:

- **Solve a Real Problem:** Your personal struggles can be your biggest business opportunities.
- **Know Your Numbers:** Passion is great, but it's the financials that will hook the investors.
- **Authenticity Sells:** Your unique background and expertise can be your greatest differentiator.
- **Be Flexible in Negotiations:** Kristen's willingness to adjust on equity showed she valued partnership over pride.
- **Find the Right Partner:** Sometimes, the best deal isn't about the money, but about finding someone who truly gets your vision.

Remember, in the Shark Tank and beyond, it's not just about having a good product - it's about having a good story, backed by solid numbers, with room to grow. Gently Soap didn't just pitch a product; it offered a piece of a growing market, a compelling narrative, and a chance to be part of a mission. That's a combination that's hard for any Shark to resist.

Lathering Up Success: Three Profound Business Lessons from Gently Soap

Lesson 1. "The Sensory Storytelling Paradigm"

Business Lesson: Engage multiple senses in your product presentation to create a more immersive and memorable pitch experience.

Scenario: Kristen didn't just talk about her soaps; she let the Sharks see, touch, and smell them. The visual appeal of the herb flecks, the tactile experience of handling the bars, and the subtle, natural fragrances created a multi-sensory experience that brought her pitch to life.

Entrepreneurial Application: Entrepreneurs can apply this by thinking beyond traditional visual and auditory presentations. Incorporate taste, smell, touch, or even proprioception (body awareness) into your pitch when relevant. This multi-sensory approach can make your product more tangible and your pitch more impactful, especially for products that aren't inherently visual or tech-based.

Lesson 2. "The Legacy Leverage Effect"

Business Lesson: Strategically intertwine personal heritage with product development to create a unique market position and emotional resonance.

Scenario: Kristen didn't just create soap; she infused her product with her grandparents' agricultural legacy and her own horticultural expertise. This backstory not only informed her product development but also created a compelling narrative that set Gently Soap apart in a crowded market.

Entrepreneurial Application: Entrepreneurs should look to their own backgrounds, family histories, and unique experiences as potential sources of product innovation and brand storytelling. This "legacy leverage" can provide authenticity, expertise, and emotional connection that competitors can't easily replicate.

Lesson 3. "The Empathy-to-Innovation Pipeline"

Business Lesson: Transform personal challenges into market opportunities by viewing your own struggles as a microcosm of larger, unaddressed consumer needs.

Scenario: Kristen's lifelong battle with eczema wasn't just a personal problem; it was a window into a growing market of consumers with sensitive skin. By solving her own issue, she inadvertently tapped into a much larger, underserved market.

Entrepreneurial Application: Entrepreneurs should view their personal pain points not as isolated issues, but as potential indicators of larger market gaps. This approach can lead to innovations that resonate deeply with specific consumer segments and solve real, felt needs rather than imagined ones.

These lessons demonstrate how Gently Soap's approach goes beyond simple product development. They challenge entrepreneurs to think holistically about their personal experiences, family histories, and sensory engagement as tools for innovation, market positioning, and pitch effectiveness. By doing so, entrepreneurs can create products and presentations that don't just solve problems, but tell stories, evoke emotions, and create lasting impressions.

Introduction: The Itch That Launched a Business

I've seen my fair share of entrepreneurs walk into the Shark Tank, each with their own story of inspiration. But when Kristen Dunning stepped onto that stage, her eyes gleaming with a mix of determination and vulnerability, I knew we were in for something different. This wasn't just another pitch; it was the culmination of a lifetime of discomfort, resilience, and innovation.

Imagine being three years old and watching your hair fall out due to scalp eczema. Picture walking down the aisles of every store, desperately searching for something - anything - to soothe your irritated skin, only to come up empty-handed time and time again. For Kristen, this wasn't just a hypothetical scenario; it was her daily reality.

But here's the thing about itches: sometimes, if they're persistent enough, they don't just irritate you - they inspire you.

Gently Soap isn't just another beauty product; it's a revolution bottled in a bar. Born from Kristen's personal struggle with eczema and sensitive skin, this line of botanical soaps is on a mission to bring joy back to bathing for the millions who've been left out of the luxurious skincare experience. By eliminating essential oils and synthetic fragrances - the usual culprits behind skin irritation - Gently Soap has created a product that's as kind to sensitive skin as it is to the nose.

But this isn't just a story about soap. It's a masterclass in turning personal pain into entrepreneurial gain. As we dive deeper into Kristen's journey, we'll uncover three transformative business lessons that any entrepreneur, regardless of industry, can lather up and apply:

1. The Sensory Storytelling Paradigm: How engaging multiple senses can transform your pitch from a mere presentation into an unforgettable experience.
2. The Legacy Leverage Effect: Why your family history isn't just nostalgia - it could be your secret weapon in product development and brand storytelling.
3. The Empathy-to-Innovation Pipeline: The art of alchemizing personal struggles into market-disrupting innovations.

These aren't just abstract concepts or boardroom buzzwords. They're practical, applicable strategies that Kristen used to turn her sensitive skin solution into a business that caught the eye of guest Shark Candace Nelson, leading to a $75,000 investment for 25% equity.

So, whether you're nursing your own entrepreneurial itch or looking to revolutionize your approach to business, strap in. We're about to embark on a journey that proves sometimes, the most powerful business ideas come not from market research reports or focus groups, but from our own lived experiences.

After all, if Kristen could transform a childhood of discomfort into a company that's changing the skincare game, imagine what you could do with your own personal challenges. Ready to lather up some success? Let's dive in.

Lesson 1: The Sensory Storytelling Paradigm

Picture this: You're standing in front of five of the most successful entrepreneurs in the country, pitching your life's work. Your palms are sweaty, your heart's racing, and you've got about 60 seconds to make an impression that could change your life. What do you do?

If you're Kristen Dunning of Gently Soap, you don't just tell them about your product - you let them experience it.

Engaging the Senses: How Gently Soap Turned a Pitch into an Experience

When Kristen walked into the Shark Tank, she didn't just bring a story - she brought a sensory experience. Each Shark received all four Gently Soap bars, not just to look at, but to touch, smell, and fully engage with. This wasn't just show-and-tell; it was show, tell, touch, and smell.

As the Sharks picked up the bars, you could see their expressions change. Barbara Corcoran noted the visible flecks of herbs and flowers. Candace Nelson commented on the subtle, natural scent. Even Mark Cuban, not typically known for his interest in personal care products, was engaged in the experience.

This, my friends, is the power of sensory storytelling. Kristen didn't just pitch a soap; she invited the Sharks into the world of Gently Soap. She made her product tangible, memorable, and most importantly, experiential.

The Power of Multi-Sensory Marketing

Now, you might be thinking, "That's great for soap, but my product isn't something you can smell or touch." Fair point, but stick with me here.

The principle of multi-sensory marketing isn't about literally engaging all five senses (though if you can, bonus points). It's about creating a richer, more immersive experience for your audience, regardless of what you're selling.

Studies have shown that engaging multiple senses can increase brand impact and memory by up to 70%. That's not just a marginal improvement - it's a game-changer.

Consider the Apple Store. They don't just show you products; they let you touch, play, and experience them. Or think about Starbucks - it's not just about the taste of coffee, but the sound of beans grinding, the smell wafting through the air, the feel of the warm cup in your hands.

Beyond Sight and Sound: Crafting Immersive Brand Experiences

So how do we apply this beyond products that are inherently sensory? Let's break it down:

1. **Visual**: This is the easy one. Use compelling imagery, whether it's product photos, infographics, or even just well-designed slides.
2. **Auditory**: This isn't just about what you say, but how you say it. Your tone, pacing, and even background music can set the mood.
3. **Tactile**: Can your audience touch your product? If not, can you provide samples, prototypes, or even related objects that evoke the right sensations?
4. **Olfactory**: Scent is strongly tied to memory. Even if your product doesn't have a smell, consider how scent could enhance your pitch environment.
5. **Gustatory**: While taste might seem limited to food products, think creatively. Could a flavor evoke the feeling you want associated with your brand?

Remember, the goal isn't to overwhelm, but to create a cohesive, memorable experience that brings your brand to life.

Action Plan: Developing Your Sensory Brand Strategy

Ready to apply the Sensory Storytelling Paradigm to your own brand? Here's a step-by-step action plan:

1. **Sensory Audit**: List all the sensory elements currently associated with your brand or product.

2. **Identify Gaps**: Which senses are underutilized in your current strategy?
3. **Brainstorm Sensory Elements**: For each sense, brainstorm potential elements that align with your brand values and message.
4. **Create Sensory Touchpoints**: Develop specific ways to incorporate these elements into your marketing, pitches, and customer experiences.
5. **Test and Refine**: Try out your new sensory elements and gather feedback. Refine based on responses.
6. **Integrate Across Channels**: Ensure your sensory branding is consistent across all customer touchpoints.

Remember, the goal isn't to assault the senses, but to create a harmonious, memorable experience that brings your brand story to life.

Kristen's Gently Soap didn't just tell a story about sensitive skin care - it allowed the Sharks to see, feel, and smell that story. And in doing so, she didn't just pitch a product; she invited the Sharks into an experience.

So, the next time you're preparing a pitch, don't just think about what you'll say. Think about what your audience will see, hear, feel, smell, and maybe even taste. Because in the end, people may forget what you said, but they'll remember how you made them feel - or in this case, how you made them smell.

After all, in business as in life, sometimes you've got to engage all the senses to come to your senses about a great opportunity. And who knows? Your multi-sensory approach might just help you clean up in your next pitch.

Lesson 2: The Legacy Leverage Effect

When Kristen Dunning stepped into the Shark Tank, she didn't just bring a soap company. She brought generations of agricultural wisdom, a childhood spent on an 84-acre farm in Alabama, and a deep understanding of the power of plants. This wasn't just backstory—it was her secret weapon.

Roots That Run Deep: Turning Family History into Market Advantage

In a world where brands often feel mass-produced and impersonal, Kristen's story struck a chord. Her grandparents' farm wasn't just a place she visited; it was the seedbed of her expertise and the root of her product's authenticity.

But here's the kicker: Kristen didn't just passively inherit this legacy. She actively transformed it into a market advantage. By leveraging her family's agricultural background, she created a product that wasn't just another soap—it was a piece of history, a continuation of a legacy, and a bridge between traditional wisdom and modern needs.

This is the essence of the Legacy Leverage Effect. It's about recognizing that your history isn't just a series of anecdotes—it's a treasure trove of differentiators, expertise, and authenticity that can set you apart in a crowded market.

From Farm to Formula: The Power of Authentic Expertise

Kristen didn't stop at family history. She doubled down on her legacy by pursuing degrees in agricultural communication and horticulture. This wasn't just about padding a resume—it was about deepening her authentic expertise.

When Kristen talked about her "proprietary herbal infusions," it wasn't marketing jargon. It was the result of years of study, three years in greenhouses, and a lifetime of connection to the land. This level of expertise isn't something you can fake or quickly acquire. It's a powerful differentiator in a market flooded with mass-produced alternatives.

The lesson? Your background isn't just where you came from—it's the unique lens through which you view your industry. It's the expertise that no one else can replicate because no one else has lived your life.

Storytelling as Brand Differentiation

In the Tank, Kristen didn't just recite facts about sensitive skin or list ingredients. She told a story—her story. From her childhood struggles with eczema to her grandparents' farm, every element wove together to create a narrative that was uniquely Gently Soap.

This isn't just good TV—it's powerful branding. In a world where consumers are bombarded with marketing messages, authentic stories cut through the noise. They create emotional connections, build trust, and make your brand memorable.

But here's the crucial part: Kristen's story wasn't separate from her product; it was integral to it. The story explained why Gently Soap exists, why it's formulated the way it is, and why Kristen was the perfect person to create it.

This is the pinnacle of the Legacy Leverage Effect. When your story isn't just a marketing tactic, but the very reason your product exists, you've created a brand that's nearly impossible to replicate.

Exercise: Mapping Your Legacy Assets

Ready to uncover the golden nuggets in your own backstory? Let's dive into a practical exercise to map out your legacy assets:

1. **Family Tree of Skills**: Draw out your family tree, but instead of names, write down the skills, trades, or knowledge areas of each family member. What patterns do you see?
2. **Personal Journey Timeline**: Create a timeline of your life, noting pivotal experiences, challenges overcome, and skills acquired. How do these relate to your business?
3. **Cultural Heritage Inventory**: List elements of your cultural background. How might these influence your approach to business or product development?
4. **Passion-to-Product Connection**: Write down your top three passions. How could these intersect with your business idea or existing product?
5. **Unique Expertise Audit**: What do you know that few others in your industry do? How did you gain this knowledge?
6. **Story Arc Development**: Using the elements you've uncovered, craft a 2-minute story that connects your personal journey to your business. Practice telling it to friends and gauge their reaction.

Remember, the goal isn't to fabricate a story, but to uncover the authentic connections between your history and your business that already exist.

The Legacy Leverage Effect isn't about living in the past—it's about recognizing that your history is a unique differentiator in a world of mass production and faceless corporations. Kristen Dunning didn't just create a soap company; she bottled generations of wisdom, personal struggle, and authentic expertise into every bar.

So, the next time you're tempted to downplay your background or consider it irrelevant to your business, remember Gently Soap. Your legacy isn't baggage to be shed on the road to success—it might just be the very thing that sets you apart and propels you forward.

After all, in the world of business, sometimes the most powerful way to clean up is to embrace where you came from. Now, isn't that a beautiful bit of alchemy?

Lesson 3: The Empathy-to-Innovation Pipeline

When Kristen Dunning shared her story of childhood eczema in the Shark Tank, it wasn't just a sob story designed to tug at our heartstrings. It was the origin story of a business built on a foundation of personal pain and hard-won empathy. This, my friends, is the Empathy-to-Innovation Pipeline in action.

Personal Pain Points as Market Research

Imagine spending your childhood unable to use fun, fragrant bath products because your skin erupts in painful rashes. Imagine walking down aisles of colorful soaps and bubble baths, knowing none of them are for you. This wasn't just Kristen's childhood - it was her market research.

Every itch, every rash, every disappointed walk through a beauty aisle was a data point. Every failed product she tried was a lesson in what the market was missing. Kristen didn't need to commission an expensive market research study to understand the needs of people with sensitive skin - she lived it.

This is the power of personal pain points. They provide a depth of understanding that no focus group or survey can match. They give you insight not just into what customers say they want, but what they truly need.

From Self-Solution to Mass Market Appeal

Here's where it gets interesting. Kristen didn't just create a product for herself. She recognized that her problem was shared by millions. Remember that statistic she dropped? 71% of the population has sensitive skin, up from 55% just two decades ago.

This is the crucial leap in the Empathy-to-Innovation Pipeline. It's not enough to solve your own problem - you need to recognize when your personal solution has mass market potential.

Kristen's journey from a little girl with eczema to the founder of a company that's changing the skincare game is a masterclass in this transition. She took her personal solution - botanical soaps free from irritating essential oils and fragrances - and scaled it into a product with broad appeal.

The Rise of the Problem-Solving Entrepreneur

Kristen's story is part of a larger trend - the rise of the problem-solving entrepreneur. These are founders who don't start with a business idea, but with a problem they're passionate about solving.

Think about it. Spanx was born because Sara Blakely couldn't find the right undergarments. Airbnb started because the founders couldn't afford their rent and needed a way to make extra money. These entrepreneurs didn't set out to disrupt industries - they set out to solve problems they intimately understood.

This approach to entrepreneurship has several advantages:

1. Deep understanding of the customer's needs
2. Passion that fuels persistence through tough times
3. Authenticity that resonates with customers
4. Firsthand experience for product testing and iteration

The problem-solving entrepreneur doesn't just create products; they create solutions. And in a world full of me-too products and copycat businesses, solutions are what stand out.

Checklist: Validating Your Personal Problem as a Market Opportunity

Ready to turn your personal pain point into the next big thing? Here's a checklist to help you validate your problem as a market opportunity:

1. **Quantify the Problem**
   - How many people share your problem?
   - Is the number growing or shrinking?
   - What's the potential market size?
2. **Analyze Existing Solutions**
   - What solutions currently exist?
   - How well do they solve the problem?
   - What's missing from these solutions?
3. **Assess Your Unique Insight**
   - What do you understand about the problem that others might miss?
   - How does your experience give you an edge in solving it?
4. **Test Your Solution**
   - Does your solution work for you consistently?
   - Have you tested it with others who share the problem?
   - How do they respond?
5. **Evaluate Scalability**
   - Can your solution be produced at scale?
   - Are the materials/technology needed readily available?
   - Can you maintain quality as you scale?
6. **Consider Pricing and Profitability**
   - What would people pay for your solution?
   - Can you produce it profitably at that price point?
   - Is there room for healthy margins?
7. **Identify Potential Obstacles**
   - What regulatory hurdles might you face?

- Are there patent or intellectual property concerns?
- What might prevent people from adopting your solution?
8. **Gauge Long-term Potential**
   - Is this a lasting problem or a temporary trend?
   - How might the problem or solution evolve over time?
   - Are there opportunities for expansion or pivots built into your idea?

Remember, not every personal problem is a business opportunity. But if you can check most of these boxes, you might just be onto something big.

The Empathy-to-Innovation Pipeline isn't just a feel-good story - it's a powerful business model. It turns personal struggles into market insights, pain points into profit centers, and empathy into innovation.

Kristen Dunning didn't just create a soap company. She turned years of frustration and discomfort into a solution that's bringing joy and relief to people just like her. And in doing so, she didn't just change her own life - she created a business that's changing lives across the country.

So the next time you find yourself frustrated by a problem, don't just complain about it. Ask yourself: Could this be my Gently Soap moment? Could this personal pain point be the beginning of your own entrepreneurial journey?

After all, in the world of business, sometimes the best way to clean up is to dig deep into the dirt of your own experiences. Now, isn't that a refreshing perspective?

Refined Pitch: Gently Soap 2.0

Before: The Original Shark Tank Pitch

"Hi Sharks, my name is Kristen Dunning and I'm a recent MBA grad from Athens, Georgia. Today I'm here seeking a $75,000 investment for a 10% equity stake in my company, Gently Soap. Sharks, humans deserve to feel joy, and no one should be robbed of joy because of their sensitive skin.

I've had eczema my entire life, and because of that, bath products would cause my skin extreme pain. Bath bombs, soaps, and bubble baths would make my skin feel like, ah! Because they were full of additives and chemicals.

I thought I was doomed to a single bar of boring white soap for the rest of my life. So, I set out to create a joyful yet gentle bathing experience for people like me, rooted in the agricultural legacy of my grandparents. I spent three years in greenhouses studying horticulture to learn more about the power of plants.

Harnessing that power, I created Gently Soap, a line of bath products that eliminates essential oils and synthetic fragrances, the stuff that causes serious irritations but still maintains an incredible gentle aroma. People with ultra-sensitive skin finally have a choice and can indulge in light and clean botanical soaps that are ultra-gentle, more sustainable, and filled with joy. It's not just for people with sensitive skin, it's for everybody.

So, Sharks, who would like to help me in completely washing away the bathing industry expectations as we know it?"

After: A Reimagined Pitch Incorporating Our Business Lessons

[Kristen enters the Shark Tank, carrying a vintage suitcase. She's wearing a lab coat over a dress made from a fabric that mimics the texture and patterns of her soap.]

"Sharks, close your eyes for a moment. Imagine being a child, watching your hair fall out due to eczema, feeling the sting of every bath, the disappointment of every beauty aisle. Now, open your eyes and join me on a sensory journey that's about to revolutionize the $20 billion sensitive skincare market.

I'm Kristen Dunning, founder of Gently Soap, and I'm here seeking $75,000 for 10% equity in a company that's not just about clean skin, but about bringing joy back to bathing for the 71% of Americans with sensitive skin.

[Kristen opens the vintage suitcase, revealing an array of Gently Soap products arranged like a miniature garden. She hands each Shark a warm, damp towel infused with the scent of her bestselling lavender soap.]

As you inhale the subtle aroma from those towels, you're experiencing more than just a scent. You're breathing in three generations of agricultural wisdom, cultivated on my grandparents' 84-acre farm in Alabama. You're sensing the result of my three years in greenhouses, studying horticulture to harness the gentle power of plants.

[Kristen removes her lab coat, fully revealing her soap-textured dress.]

This dress represents the unique, visual appeal of our soaps. Like this fabric, each Gently Soap bar is a work of art, with visible herbs and flowers that signal its natural origin to our customers.

But Gently Soap isn't just about looking or smelling good. It's about feeling good - really good. Our proprietary herbal infusions eliminate the need for harsh essential oils and synthetic fragrances, delivering a truly gentle experience for even the most sensitive skin.

[Kristen hands each Shark a Gently Soap bar.]

Feel the texture. See the natural ingredients. Experience the subtle fragrance. This isn't just a product; it's a solution born from my lifelong struggle with eczema, refined through years of research, and perfected with the wisdom of generations.

In just two years, we've generated $113,000 in sales, with a whopping 78% repeat customer rate. Our customer acquisition cost is just $5.83, with an average order value of $42.38. And with 60% of our customers suffering from skin conditions like eczema and psoriasis, we're not just selling soap - we're delivering relief, confidence, and joy.

Sharks, I'm not here to just disrupt the bathing industry. I'm here to heal it, to bring empathy and innovation to a market that's been neglecting millions of sensitive-skinned individuals for far too long.

So, who's ready to dive in and make waves in the skincare industry with Gently Soap?"

Conclusion: From Sensitive Skin to Sensitive Business

As we rinse off the last suds of our deep dive into Gently Soap's journey, it's clear that Kristen Dunning has done more than just create a skincare product. She's crafted a blueprint for turning personal struggles into business triumphs, and in doing so, has offered us a masterclass in empathy-driven entrepreneurship.

Recap of Key Lessons from Gently Soap's Journey

1. **The Sensory Storytelling Paradigm**: Kristen showed us that in a world drowning in digital noise, engaging multiple senses can create a pitch that's not just heard, but felt. By allowing the Sharks to see, touch, and smell her product, she transformed her pitch from a mere presentation into an immersive experience. In your own ventures, remember that your audience isn't just listening - they're experiencing. How can you make that experience unforgettable?
2. **The Legacy Leverage Effect**: Through Gently Soap, we learned that our backgrounds aren't baggage, but a treasure trove of unique selling points. Kristen's family farm wasn't just a childhood memory; it was the root of her expertise and the soul of her brand. What aspects of your own history might you be

overlooking? Your next big idea might be hiding in plain sight, nestled in the stories you've known all your life.

3. **The Empathy-to-Innovation Pipeline**: Perhaps most powerfully, Kristen demonstrated that our deepest struggles can be wellsprings of innovation. Her lifelong battle with eczema wasn't just a personal challenge; it was unintentional market research that led to a product serving millions. What problems do you intimately understand? That understanding could be your ticket to creating solutions that resonate deeply with others who share your struggles.

The Future of Empathy-Driven Entrepreneurship

As we look to the horizon, it's clear that the future of business isn't just about profit margins and market share. It's about connection, understanding, and genuine problem-solving. Gently Soap isn't just a company; it's a harbinger of a new way of doing business - one that places empathy at the core of innovation.

In a world where consumers are increasingly seeking authenticity and purpose in their purchases, empathy-driven entrepreneurs like Kristen have a distinct advantage. They're not just selling products; they're offering solutions born from real understanding and personal experience.

This shift towards empathy-driven entrepreneurship isn't just good for consumers; it's good for business. It leads to products that solve real problems, brands that connect on a deeper level, and companies that make a genuine difference in people's lives.

Call to Action for Aspiring Entrepreneurs

So, to all you aspiring entrepreneurs out there, here's my challenge to you:

1. **Embrace Your Story**: Your experiences, even the painful ones, are not liabilities. They're assets. They're the unique lens through which you see the world, and they could be the foundation of your next big idea.
2. **Solve Real Problems**: Don't just chase trends or try to build a better mousetrap. Look for the problems that keep people up at night, the ones that affect quality of life. Those are the problems worth solving, and they're the solutions people will pay for.
3. **Engage All Senses**: In a world of endless pitches and presentations, find ways to stand out by creating experiences. Whether you're pitching to investors or selling to customers, engage as many senses as you can.
4. **Lead with Empathy**: Understanding your customer isn't just about market research. It's about genuinely caring about their problems and being passionate about solving them.
5. **Leverage Your Legacy**: Your background, your family history, your unique experiences - these aren't just anecdotes. They're differentiators. Use them to create a brand and a product that no one else could.

Remember, every bar of Gently Soap started with a little girl who just wanted to enjoy a bath without pain. Your next big idea might be hiding in your own story, waiting for you to recognize its potential.

In the end, business isn't just about transactions; it's about transformations. Kristen Dunning didn't just create a soap company; she created a vehicle for bringing joy back to people who thought they'd lost it. That's the power of empathy-driven entrepreneurship.

So, as you embark on your own entrepreneurial journey, ask yourself: What's your Gently Soap? What problem do you understand so deeply that you're uniquely positioned to solve it? Find that, and you might just change the world - and wash away some outdated notions about business in the process.

After all, in the grand bath of entrepreneurship, it's not just about making a splash. It's about creating ripples that can cleanse an entire industry. Now, isn't that a business idea worth lathering up for?

The Gently Soap Startup Bootcamp

Welcome to the Gently Soap Startup Bootcamp! Here, we'll turn theory into practice with four hands-on exercises designed to help you uncover your own entrepreneurial potential. Grab a notebook, open your mind, and let's dive in!

1. "Sensory Mapping Exercise": Identify unique sensory elements in your product/service

Objective: Develop a multi-sensory brand experience that captivates your audience.

Exercise:

1. Draw a large circle and divide it into five sections, one for each sense.
2. In each section, brainstorm how your product/service could engage that sense:
   - Sight: What unique visual elements does your product have?
   - Sound: Is there a signature sound associated with your product or its use?
   - Touch: What textures or physical sensations are part of your product experience?
   - Smell: Are there any scents, natural or added, that define your product?
   - Taste: Even for non-food items, is there a taste element or association?

3. For each sense, rate the current engagement level from 1-5.
4. Identify the two lowest-rated senses and brainstorm three ways to enhance engagement for each.
5. Create a "sensory tagline" that incorporates at least three senses.

Reflection: How could enhancing these sensory elements differentiate your product in the market?

2. "Legacy Mining Workshop": Uncover valuable assets in your personal/family history

Objective: Discover unique elements of your background that could inform or enhance your business.

Exercise:

1. Create a "legacy map" by drawing a tree with three main branches: Family History, Personal Experiences, and Cultural Background.
2. On each branch, write down key elements:
   - Family History: Occupations, skills, traditions, stories
   - Personal Experiences: Education, travel, challenges overcome, unique skills
   - Cultural Background: Values, customs, language, art forms
3. Circle the three elements that resonate most with you.
4. For each circled element, answer:

- How does this make me or my perspective unique?
- What special insight or skill does this give me?
- How could this inform or enhance a business idea?

5. Write a short "legacy statement" incorporating these elements and how they shape your entrepreneurial vision.

Reflection: How can you authentically integrate these elements into your brand story?

3. "Empathy-to-Innovation Challenge": Transform a personal struggle into a business idea

Objective: Identify a personal pain point and develop it into a viable business concept.

Exercise:

1. List three personal challenges you've faced or are facing.
2. For each challenge, answer:
   - Who else might share this problem?
   - What existing solutions have you tried? Why weren't they satisfactory?
   - What would an ideal solution look like?
3. Choose the challenge with the most potential and create an "empathy map":
   - What does someone with this problem think and feel?
   - What do they hear? What do they say and do?

- What are their pain points? What would they gain from a solution?
4. Brainstorm three possible solutions to this challenge.
5. For your favorite solution, outline:
    - Key features
    - Target market
    - Potential revenue streams
    - Unique selling proposition

Reflection: How does your personal experience with this challenge give you a competitive edge?

4. "Multi-Sensory Pitch Deck": Create a pitch that engages all five senses

Objective: Develop a pitch presentation that creates an immersive, memorable experience.

Exercise:

1. Outline a basic 5-slide pitch deck for your business idea.
2. For each slide, brainstorm how you could engage each sense:
    - Sight: Beyond text and images, what visual elements could you incorporate?
    - Sound: What audio could enhance your message?
    - Touch: What tangible elements could you include?
    - Smell: How could you incorporate relevant scents?
    - Taste: Could you include a taste element, even if your product isn't edible?
3. Create a "sensory storyboard" mapping out these elements alongside your key points.
4. Develop a "pitch kit" - a collection of items that engage multiple senses and reinforce your message.
5. Practice delivering your pitch using your sensory elements. Time it and ensure it stays under 5 minutes.

Reflection: How does this multi-sensory approach make your pitch more memorable and impactful?

Remember, the goal of these exercises isn't perfection, but exploration and discovery. You're not just developing a product or service; you're crafting an experience, telling a story, and solving real problems.

So, lather up that creativity, rinse away self-doubt, and let's see what amazing ideas you can conjure up. After all, if Kristen Dunning could turn her struggle with eczema into a successful business that caught a Shark's attention, imagine what you could do with your unique experiences and insights.

Now, go forth and let your entrepreneurial spirit gently (but effectively) cleanse the market of lackluster ideas. Your Gently Soap moment awaits!

Are You Ready To Become Shark Savvy?

We invite you to subscribe to our Free Newsletter - The Shark Savvy Stoic. 3 times a week (Monday, Wednesday, and Friday) we send you some savvy wisdom that we have uncovered during our Shark Tank Pitch evaluations. And if you join us today we will include a digital copy of The Entrepreneur's Eureka: A 5-Question Interactive Workbook. Dive into the minds of Shark Tank's most successful investors with this powerful, interactive workbook. Uncover the five critical questions that can turn any business scenario into a goldmine of insights. Inside, you'll find:

- A step-by-step framework to analyze business situations like a pro
- Real-world examples from Shark Tank's biggest success stories
- Practical exercises to immediately apply to your own ventures
- A self-assessment tool to measure your "Shark Savvy" quotient
- An action plan template to turn insights into tangible results turn insights into tangible results

Join Us Here: https://sharksavvy.com/s15e1

Shark Savvy: The Tank-Tested Playbook for Entrepreneurial Domination Book Series

https://www.amazon.com/gp/product/B0DCH21VC9

by Shark Savvy (Author) , Jimmy Slagle (Author)

Welcome to the Shark Savvy series, where we turn Shark Tank episodes into your personal MBA program—minus the soul-crushing debt and questionable cafeteria food.

Picture this: You're lounging on your couch, binge-watching Shark Tank, when suddenly you realize you've learned more about business in one hour than you did in four years of college. That's the Shark Savvy experience, but on steroids (the legal kind, we promise).

Each book in this groundbreaking series takes a deep dive into a single Shark Tank episode, extracting the juiciest, most mind-blowing business lessons that most entrepreneurs miss while they're distracted by Mr. Wonderful's dazzling bald head. We're talking real, actionable insights that you can apply to your business faster than Mark Cuban can say, "I'm out."

But wait, there's more! (Yes, we went there.) These books aren't just educational—they're more entertaining than watching Kevin O'Leary try to dance. We've infused each page with wit sharper than Lori Greiner's negotiation skills and wisdom more profound than Daymond John's fashion sense.

Here's what you're in for with each Shark Savvy book:

6. A blow-by-blow analysis of a Shark Tank pitch that'll make you feel like you're right there in the Tank (minus the intimidating cameras and Barbara Corcoran's penetrating stare).
7. Mind-bending business lessons that'll have you slapping your forehead and saying, "Why didn't I think of that?" (Don't slap too hard; we need your brain cells intact.)
8. Practical exercises that'll whip your entrepreneurial muscles into shape faster than you can say "royalty deal."
9. Real-world applications that'll help you swim with the sharks instead of becoming chum.
10. A healthy dose of Stoic philosophy, because nothing says "I'm a serious entrepreneur" like quoting Marcus Aurelius while pitching your avocado toast food truck.

But here's the kicker: Each book stands alone as a complete guide to entrepreneurial badassery. However, collect them all, and you'll have a library of business wisdom more valuable than a 20% stake in Amazon circa 1997.

So, why should you buy every book in the Shark Savvy series? Because in the cutthroat world of business, you need every advantage you can get. It's like Pokemon for entrepreneurs—gotta catch 'em all if you want to be the very best (like no one ever was).

Whether you're a seasoned business owner looking to up your game or a wide-eyed newbie who thinks a "liquidation event" involves spring break in Cancun, the Shark Savvy series has something for you. Each book is a treasure trove of lessons, laughs, and "let's do this" motivation that'll have you revamping your business plan before you've even finished the epilogue.

Don't let your entrepreneurial dreams become the one that got away. Dive into the Shark Savvy series and start your journey from guppy to great white today. Remember, in the vast ocean of business, it's eat or be eaten—and we're serving up a feast of knowledge that's sure to satisfy even the hungriest of entrepreneurs.

So what are you waiting for? Grab your scuba gear (or just your reading glasses) and plunge into the Shark Savvy series. Your future self—you know, the one sipping margaritas on your private island—will thank you.

Shark Savvy: Because why learn from your own mistakes when you can learn from someone else's on national television?

Want to go even Deeper? Check out SharkSavvy.com and Dive Into The Depths of Success!

www.ingramcontent.com/pod-product-compliance
Lightning Source LLC
Chambersburg PA
CBHW071831210526
45479CB00001B/86